# KAR

# THE UPRIV          LE

### By
### Maureen Bell

Naturegraph Publishers, Inc.

**Library of Congress Cataloging in Publication Data**

Bell, Maureen, 1962-
Karuk: The Upriver People / by Maureen Bell.
  p.    cm.
Includes bibliographical references.


ISBN 0-87961-208-8
ISBN 0-87961-209-6 (paper)
  1. Karuk Indians.    I. Title
E99.K25B45    1991
979.4'1004975--dc20                              91-29066
                                                    CIP

Cover painting by Ralph Starritt
Cover design by Albert Vanderhoof

**Naturegraph Publishers, Inc.**
3543 Indian Creek Road
Happy Camp, CA 96039
U.S.A.

# Preface

This book about the Karuk Indians of northwestern California integrates for the first time material from many different ethnological and local sources that have never appeared under one cover before. I extend special appreciation to such early researchers in the field of Karuk ethnology as A. L. Kroeber, Edward Curtis, Edward W. Gifford, John Harrington, and William Bright, from whose works I have borrowed extensively. An even deeper appreciation belongs to those Karuk informants who gave freely to the anthropologists their knowledge of the traditional Karuk ways, thus preserving them from irretrievable loss.

The following questions shall be considered in this work: What have archaeologists discovered about the prehistoric world of the Karuk and the middle course of the Klamath River which they inhabit? Who were the Karuk and what was their lifestyle and habitation like when the earliest miners and new settlers first immigrated into the Klamath River region in the early 1850s? How were the Karuk treated by the newcomers? What changes have occurred in the Karuk cultural and social lifestyle? Whatever answers are given herein, the reader should remember that our knowledge of aboriginal cultures is never exact, that our speculations based upon the information given by informants and archaeological remains are hypothetical models, not absolute facts. The reader is encouraged to consult the bibliography at the end of this book to undertake deeper research into the history and ways of the Upriver People.

# Table of Contents

# Chapter 1

# INTRODUCING THE KARUK-ARARA

For an unknown number of generations, the Upriver People, or Karuk-arara, secured their homes and villages along the middle course of the Klamath River in northwestern California. This region is located between the Coastal Mountains to the west and the Cascade Range to the east. The heartland of California lies to the south and, to the north, after crossing the steep and rugged Siskiyou Mountains, are the hamlets of Jackson County, Oregon.

Separate Indian groups bordered the Karuk on all sides. Downriver, and within a radius of six miles, three of the six major linguistic groups recognized in North America came into contact, sharing a similar culture. The Hupa, who spoke Athabascan, lived along the Trinity River south of the Karuk, while the Yurok-arara, or Downriver People, who spoke Algonkian, resided on the Klamath just below and to the southwest of the Karuk. The ancient hunting grounds of the Tolowa were to the northwest, above the watersheds of Bluff Creek. The Shasta, who spoke a similar Hokan language to the Karuk, lived to the east. Extinct groups who once lived nearby include the New River Shasta, the Kammat-wa, the Watiru, and the Konomihu.

Despite linguistic differences, the most closely interrelated groups were the Karuk, Hupa, and Yurok—or the "Klamath River Indians."[1] Many of their laws, customs, and values were similar, and a large trade network existed between them. They also participated in each others religious ceremonies and intermarried.

The Shasta had less contact with the Upriver People than the Hupa and Yurok, as some of their villages were separated by large mountain barriers. However, they did exchange goods with the Klamath River Indians.

## Origin of the Klamath Mountains[2]

During the Jurassic period (190-136 M.Y.B.P.), when dinosaurs were flourishing and the first birds and mammals began to appear, shallow seas covered large areas of the western United States. In what was to become northwestern California, two crustal plates, one under North America and one under the Pacific, collided and began thrusting up the Klamath Mountains as well as the Sierras and the coastal mountains of Oregon. This geological activity lasted for a long period of time, during which the mountains began to be reduced by erosion. At last, by the Paleocene period, when dinosaurs had disappeared, the Klamath Mountains were a region of broad valleys and gently rolling hills bordering a subtropical sea.

At this time (about thirty million years ago) another period of tectonic activity began along the Pacific Coast. It separated the Klamath-Sierra range by bending the Klamaths westward while throwing up the vast Modoc Plateau in between. The sideways rubbing of the two plates split them into large fault blocks, many of which were pushed up to become steep mountain slopes. By two or three million years ago the Klamaths and the Sierras looked much like they do today. Weather and glaciers continued to carve their jagged peaks and deep canyons. Inland streams worked their way through these mountain blockades to create such water outlets as the Klamath, Salmon, and Trinity rivers.

About one million to five hundred thousand years ago, the giant mammoth appeared in northwestern California. Fossils of a mammoth have been unearthed from nearby Mt. Shasta in the Shasta Valley, giving evidence that these early mammals roamed throughout this region at this time.

During the Ice Age, or Pleistocene epoch, the physical formation of the Klamath Mountains was completed. Several of its large peaks were swept with glaciers. During the time of the last glaciation, there were at least thirty alpine valley glaciers up to thirteen miles long in the Klamath Mountains.[3]

Mammoths, ground sloths, horses, camels, saber-toothed cats, and giant wolves were among the many now extinct animals that roamed northern California during the late Ice Age or early Holocene epoch. At about the same time, the first human inhabitants of northern California, of whom we are presently aware, migrated into the area. They were primarily hunters following the great Pleistocene herds. As the herds began to diminish, the gathering of plant food became more important.

## Archaeology

Archaeologists can only speculate as to when the Karuk, or their Hokan-speaking ancestors, first arrived in the Klamath River region. The terrain there attracts the harsh, moist climate of the Pacific, causing materials to erode quickly and easily, removing much of the evidence of ancient habitation. The material cultures of the region were also exceedingly similar, although their languages differed greatly. Therefore, accurate archaeological conclusions are difficult to arrive at.

The first occupants of the region were probably Hokan-speakers. This stock is believed to be among the oldest in California because its members were so widely scattered geographically.[4] Tribes such as the Karuk, Chimariko, Pomo, Shastan, Yana, and the Washoe, as well as a few groups residing in southern California and on the Santa Catalina Islands belong to this linguistic family. This could be evidence that the ancestors of the Karuk were among the first to enter the "golden state."

During Paleolithic times beginning more than ten thousand years ago, the Indians of ancient California migrated seasonally to take advantage of the different ripening times of wild-food sources. The movement to seasonal camps was probably part of a carefully scheduled annual round which was made, usually, from base or winter camps in the low-lands to summer camps in the mountains and high valleys. These migrating groups consisted of little more than families, who hunted and gathered along the way.[5] X-ray studies of the early skeletal remains show that these people frequently starved during the late winter months when little wild food was available. At this time their growth and reproductive abilities were impaired.[6] However, they possessed a specialized technology, since dozens of types of scrapers, refined stone tools, baskets, milling tools, ritual objects, and personal ornaments have been found among the archaeological evidence.[7]

At Borax Lake in Lake County, on an obsidian flow, was an especially important camp of this kind.[8] Although it was used for occupation, it was primarily a work station for the manufacture of numerous stone implements. Archaeologists have gathered more stone tools there than at any other Paleolithic site in California. Many of these artifacts are ten thousand to twelve thousand years old.[9]

Other sites inhabited by early northern Californians include Nightfire Island and Pilot Ridge. Seasonal waterfowl were hunted at the Nightfire Island site along the shore of Lower Klamath Lake. This site contains hunting, butchering, hide preparation, and woodworking tools, as well as grinding implements and evidence of burials and living structures dating back to as far as 4,000 B.C.[10] Pilot Ridge, south of Hoopa, revealed wide-stemmed projectile points, stone cutting and scraping tools, and milling implements similar to the ones found for the same time period at Borax Lake and other northcoast sites.[11]

A Penutian linguistic stock is believed to have entered California from the north and colonized the Central Valley around 2,000 B.C.[12] This included the ancestors of the Wintu, the Maidu, the Miwok, the Yokut, and the Modoc tribes. The Hokan speakers already present in California were probably dispersed even wider geographically by this invasion.

One of the earliest human settlements in northwestern California yet discovered is at Point Saint George, located just above Crescent City.[13] This early Pacific site, dated by radiocarbon to 310 B.C., may originally have been a small camp occupied by ancestors of the Karuk from the interior who journeyed there for flint.[14]

It is believed that the Karuk held relatively undisputed control over the northwestern California region until the Wiyot came down from the north about 900 A.D.[15] Because the Wiyot settled on the coastal strip, an area little used by the Karuk, their entry did not place much stress on the Karuk lifeways.

The Yurok entered California from the north about two hundred years after the Wiyot and introduced new methods of fishing, as well as preservation and storage. They also brought their woodworking skills, for which the Pacific Northwest Indians are famous. After the Yurok arrived, the Karuk adopted these technologies and shifted from depending primarily on hunting and gathering to a more riverine culture.[16]

The coming of the Algonkian-speaking Wiyot and Yurok into northwestern California marks the beginning of the so-called Gunther Pattern. This pattern, which is named after Gunther Island just west of Eureka in Wiyot territory, includes such assemblages as harpoon points, woodworking tools, dentalium shells, and other distinctive artifacts of the coastal and riverine culture.[17]

Another wave of newcomers to the region were members of the Athabascan language family, ancestors of the Hupa and the Tolowa. They came from the northern interior as late as 1300 A.D. and were used to an interior forested environment. The sinew-backed bow may have been one of their contributions to the Northwestern California Culture.[18]

According to evidence unearthed at Iron Gate Reservoir and Seiad Valley, the earliest settlement in that part of the Klamath River began between 600 to 1000 A.D. Although the routes traveled by the immigrants and the dates of their arrival in northwestern California are speculative, it is certain that peoples with widely different languages settled in the region around one thousand years ago. Despite linguistic differences, these peoples soon came to have similar social, economic, and religious values.[19]

# Endnotes

1. A. L. Kroeber, *Handbook of the Indians of California*, p. 98.

2. Information on the origin of the Klamath Mountains is derived from David R. Wallace, *The Klamath Knot*, pp. 23-25.

3. Gordon B. Oakeshott, *California's Changing Landscapes*, p. 267.

4. Michael J. Moratto, *California Archaeology*, p. 536.

5. Joseph L. Chartkoff and Kerry K. Chartkoff, *The Archaeology of California*, pp. 74-77.

6. Ibid., p. 139.

7. Ibid., pp. 77-78.

8. Ibid., p. 52.

9. C. W. Meighan and C. V. Haynes, "The Borax Lake Site Revisited," *Science*, vol. 167, no. 3922, pp. 1213-1221.

10. Michael J. Moratto, *California Archaeology*, p. 461.

11. Ibid., p. 492.

12. Ibid., p. 539.

13. Richard A. Gould, *A Radiocarbon Date from Point St. George Site, Northwestern California*, Contributions of the University of California Archaeological Research Facility, vol. 14, pp. 41-44.

14. Michael J. Moratto, *California Archaeology*, pp. 481-483.

15. Ibid., p. 483.

16. Ibid.

17. Ibid, p. 484.

18. Ibid.

19. Joseph L. Chartkoff and Kerry K. Chartkoff, *The Archaeology of California*, p. 201.

# Chapter 2

# GEOGRAPHY

The mountains of the Klamath and Six Rivers National Forest that surround Karuk country are lush, with more vegetation and precipitation than the Sierra Nevada. They serve as a barrier for moisture-laden winds blowing in from the Pacific. These winds cause a Mediterranean-type climate, marked by heavy rains in the winter and dry, warm summers. The rainfall averages fifty to sixty inches annually, creating many waterways.

## Streams and Creeks

The Karuk world focused upon the Klamath and Salmon rivers. Their national boundary followed the watersheds of the Klamath and they held fishing rights halfway up to the Forks of the Salmon. These streams are protected by the Federal Wild and Scenic River System.

The Klamath River, the largest stream to enter the Pacific Ocean between the Sacramento to the south and the Columbia to the north, was so vital to the Karuk that it served as the basis for their spatial orientation. The four cardinal directions were: *yuruk*, or downriver; *karuk*, or upriver; *maruk*, meaning away from the river or uphill; and *saruk*, meaning toward the river or downhill.[1]

The Klamath River stretches for 263 miles, beginning in south-central Oregon, where it journeys southwest through swampy high country. When it enters the Klamath Canyon, its rapids break over rocky ledges and boulders as it passes through the rugged slopes and narrow valleys of the Klamath Mountains. After following this route for more than one hundred miles, it finally flows into the Pacific Ocean in northwestern California.

The north fork of the Salmon River begins in the Marble Mountains, and its south fork starts in the Salmon-Trinity Alps. These brilliantly blue waters rush downslope, wash over huge boulders and fallen logs, and finally meet at the Forks of the Salmon. They then journey through steep canyons and heavily forested terrain. Where Wooley Creek tumbles into the Salmon's mighty rapids, the river descends another five miles until it plunges into the Klamath River at Somes Bar. The Salmon River is so loud that people must shout to hear each other above its roar and rumble. Its whirling waters cause eddies and fling brush and tree trunks against its jagged stones.

Numerous creeks and small streams flow down the mountain slopes to feed these rivers, which support large numbers of trout, steelhead, and salmon.

## Karuk Villages

Villages once extended for a sixty mile stretch from just below Seiad Valley to a rocky pass on Bluff Creek, about seven miles below Orleans.[2] Most bordered the Klamath River, but some dotted the Salmon and other tributaries. The Karuk considered Ka'tim'iin, an ancient ceremonial site on the Klamath River just above the mouth of the Salmon, the center of their world.[3]

When A. L. Kroeber visited the Karuk around the turn of the century, he identified three principal population clusters, each consisting of a major ceremonial site with smaller villages nearby. These were as follows: 1) Panámniik, located near the mouth of Camp Creek; 2) Ka'tim'iin, located above the mouth of the Salmon River; and 3) Inaam, located near the mouth of Clear Creek. Other stretches of the Klamath held additional Karuk villages.[4] Although miners burned many Karuk villages in 1852, there were still over ninety left in the late 1860s.

The major towns in Karuk country today are found along the Klamath River Highway in Siskiyou and Humboldt counties. This curvy and isolated road follows the Klamath River and is the only low elevation crossing of the Klamath Mountains. Below follow descriptions of a few of the more important Karuk sites and corresponding modern towns.[5] (For a complete list of 117 known village sites refer to the appendix of William Bright's *The Karok Language*.) Visitors to these sites should remember that these places are sacred to the Karuk and must be respected and left undisturbed.

**Seiad Valley.** *Seiad* is a Karuk word meaning peaceful. This tiny town is far upriver from the majority of Karuk village sites and borders on Shasta territory. A farmer named Reeves from New York, who bought most of Seiad Valley after it was settled by Americans, made a fortune here by supplying meat and produce to the miners along the Klamath. The first school in Seiad Valley was established in 1872.[6]

**'Athithúfvuunupma.** 'Athithúfvuunupma was a Karuk village at the mouth of Indian Creek. It is now the town of Happy Camp. This town is located on the west bank of the Klamath River and is surrounded on all sides by mountains with sparkling streams. Legend has it that Happy Camp derived its modern name after a group of miners found gold there in 1852.[7] The miners became exuberant and, while passing a bottle of spirits around to celebrate the find, one of them looked around the camp, saw everyone smiling, and said, "Boy! This sure is a happy camp!" Thus, the new town was baptized.

**Inaam.** Situated on a small, flat stretch of land near the bridge crossing Clear Creek, about ten miles south of Happy Camp, this important village held the World Renewal Ceremony each August. It was a large town, well-known even to the Yurok.

**Píptaas.** A summer camp for drying salmon was located on the east side of the Klamath River opposite Inaam. It played an important part in the World Renewal Ceremony.

**Xuumnípaak.** This village, about halfway between the two major ceremonial centers of Inaam and Ka'tim'iin, cuddled a sparkling clear-blue creek. Now visitors to the area can enjoy this cool, secluded forest site as the Dillon Creek

Campground, while remembering that it is a sacred spot to the Karuk.

**Ka'tim'iin.** This was the Karuk's most sacred village, Thivthaneen-áachip, "the center of the world," and the most populated. It was also called Upper Dam. The Karuk held the World Renewal Ceremony here every September. Ka'tim'iin is located on a bluff, adjacent to Mt. Offield, that overlooks the swift Klamath rapids not far above the mouth of the Salmon. The modern hamlet of Somes Bar is located nearby. Miners took the site from the Karuk in the early 1850s.

**Ishi Pishi.** This was the name for a large cluster of villages surrounding some falls on the west bank of the Klamath River directly opposite of Ka'tim'iin. The Boat Dance was performed on the river here on years when the real Deerskin Dance was held.

**Sak'iripirak.** Near to Ka'tim'iin, this village was well-known because of its proximity to Sugarloaf Peak (A'uuyich), a sheer rock cliff rising out of the Klamath, which played an important part in Karuk mythology.

**Vunxirak.** This weir-building spot was located on the north bank of Oak Bottom Flat. A miner's camp once occupied this site, which is just over a mile up the Salmon River from Somes Bar and four miles below Wooley Creek. Visitors can camp here at the Oak Bottom Campground.

**Ameekyáaraam.** An important ceremonial village, this was the only site where the Karuk held the First Salmon Ceremony and the Jump Dance. Ameekyáaraam, meaning "where they make salmon," is situated on a bluff on the west bank of the Klamath River about one mile below the mouth of the Salmon. It is one of the best preserved Karuk villages.

**Asánaamkarak.** Also called Lower Dam, this site was located on the east bank of the Klamath River directly across from Ameekyáaraam and played an important part in the First Salmon Ceremony. It was once occupied by the ranch

*Photo 1. The Klamath and Salmon rivers converging in front of A'uuyich (Sugarloaf Mt.).*

of Ike, a Karuk informant to the anthropologists Kroeber and Gifford. Ike's Falls, a popular fishing spot, is located here.

**Panámniik.** This important ceremonial village was located about seven miles below the mouth of the Salmon River. The World Renewal Ceremony was held here each September simultaneously with the one in Ka'tim'íin. When miners moved into the area in the 1850s, Panámniik was partially occupied, and the new town was given the name of Orleans. It was the Klamath County seat from 1855 until 1875, during which time it was a thriving mining and lumbering community.

**Ishpúutach.** Situated on a bluff above Bluff Creek on the west bank of the Klamath about seven miles below Orleans, this site was the most downriver of all Karuk villages. Below Karuk country is the ancient homeland of the Hupa and the Yurok.

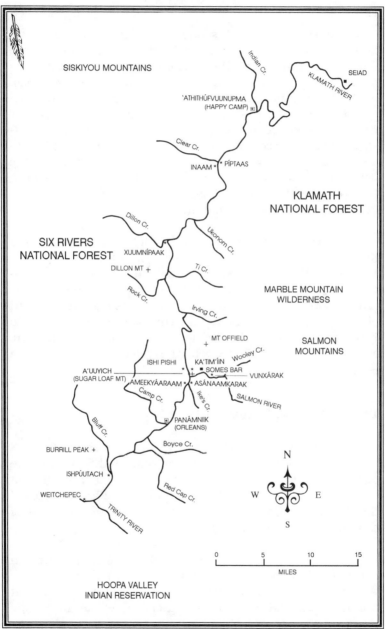

SISKIYOU MOUNTAINS

Indian Cr.

SEIAD

KLAMATH RIVER

'ATHITHÚFVUUNUPMA
(HAPPY CAMP)

Clear Cr.

INAAM * * PÍPTAAS

KLAMATH
NATIONAL FOREST

Dillon Cr.

Ukonom Cr.

SIX RIVERS
NATIONAL FOREST

XUUMNÍPAAK

DILLON MT +

Ti Cr.

Rock Cr.

MARBLE MOUNTAIN
WILDERNESS

Irving Cr.

MT OFFIELD
+

SALMON
MOUNTAINS

Wooley Cr.

ISHI PISHI

KA'TIM'ÍIN

A'UUYICH
(SUGAR LOAF MT)

SOMES BAR

VUNXÁRAK

AMEEKYÁARAAM * * ASÁNAAMKARAK

Camp Cr.

Ike's Cr.

SALMON RIVER

PANÁMNIIK
(ORLEANS)

Bluff Cr.

Boyce Cr.

N

BURRILL PEAK +

ISHPÚUTACH *

WEITCHEPEC *

Red Cap Cr.

W        E

TRINITY RIVER

S

0        5        10        15

MILES

HOOPA VALLEY
INDIAN RESERVATION

# Mountains[8]

Karuk country contains one of the greatest concentrations of mountain wilderness in the continental United States. The Karuk and their neighbors did not inhabit the high country, but they did assign a hierarchy to its slopes. In the lower lands, individuals hunted, gathered, and engaged in the numerous activities of daily living. The higher ridges were considered more sacred. Here, ceremonial leaders and doctors received extensive training, learning to create medicines as well as to recite certain prayers to the Ikxaréeyav, "the immortals" who founded the Karuk world. Groups sometimes made pilgrimages to the highest summits to honor these "ancient ones."

The metamorphic and granitic highlands surrounding Karuk country include the Siskiyou Mountains, the Marble Mountain Wilderness Area, the Red Buttes, and the northwest portion of the Salmon-Trinity Alps—all part of the Klamath Mountain region. It also includes a small segment of the Six Rivers National Forest. The peaks average 5,000 to 7,000 feet, but exceed 8,000 feet in some places. There are few flat places or gradients below forty degrees, thus the area is steep and rugged.

## The Siskiyou Mountains

Running north to northeast and east across the California-Oregon border, the rugged and glaciated Siskiyous are one of the largest blocks of wild country left in California today. This landscape, encompassing some 200,000 acres of the Klamath National Forest, forms the most northerly arc of the Klamath Mountain region.

Roads off Highway 96 lead travelers into rich mountain country where signs designate trailheads. Adventurers wishing to visit the Siskiyous can find trail information at the Klamath National Forestry Service, either in Happy Camp or downriver at Ukonom.

Mount Offield, upriver from the Ukonom Ranger District and adjacent to Ka'tim'iin, is the most sacred mountain in Karuk country. The Karuk dubbed it Ikxaréeyav Túuyship (mountain of the immortals). One Karuk woman described it as "an immortal woman whose 'hair' has to be singed so there will not be many widows and widowers in the world."[9] Every September, during the World Renewal Ceremony, or Pikyavish, at Ka'tim'iin, the Karuk would burn the brush on this slope. (This is no longer done as it was frowned upon by Anglos and outlawed in the early 1920s.) As part of the World Renewal Ceremony, the Karuk bathed before and after ascending Mt. Offield. When collecting food on the slope, the people did not eat, drink, or rest until arriving at Turtle Lake, midway up the slope at 2,000 feet. People ate and drank only after bathing in the lake, for the Ikxaréeyav so ordained it. According to tradition, the Karuk could not mention death nor have burials on this mountain, or protracted rains would follow.

Bear Peak trailhead at Inaam is another location in the Siskiyous where the Karuk held the Pikyavish. The trail marker to Bear Peak reads: "Bear Peak Trail - Elbow Springs." The springs are the only source of water until one reaches the first Bear Lake, three and a half miles away.

Bear Peak Trail climbs gently, yet steadily, for about three miles to Bear Peak. Dillon Divide is visible to the south. Near the trail stand varieties of rare wildflowers and such evergreens as Douglas fir and mountain hemlock, as well as kinnikinnik (a tobaccolike plant), cedar, and tan-oak.

Botanists call the Klamath Mountains the richest coniferous forest in the world, as there is such a variety and abundance of cone-bearing trees. In the Siskiyous, Bear Basin Butte near Youngs Valley has fifteen or sixteen different species of these trees in its vicinity alone.

The Alpine wilderness has many glaciated slopes, such as Bear Paw, El Capitan, and Black Butte. Long sections of the mountain crests are without trails. Here, granite walls drop into pockets, or "cirques," where little lakes have replaced glaciers. Dozens of creeks run through the forested valleys of these high spur ridges.

Preston Peak, the highest slope, rises 7,309 feet above sea level, but seems twice as high for it dominates the landscape. Looking west from Preston's summit, one can see the blue line of the mighty Pacific. The line is gray on foggy days.

Youngs Valley, near Preston Peak, is an ancient hunting ground of the Karuk, the Tolowa, and the Yurok, the primary home of the legendary Bigfoot, and the meeting place for various trails leading to Devil's Canyon, Raspberry and Island lakes, Preston Peak, and other scenic places. Devil's Canyon is exquisite, being a glacier-cut cirque with walls 1,500 feet high.

The lush Siskiyou woodlands abound with black bear, white-tailed deer, mountain lions, and wolverines. Due to their keen intelligence and ability to avoid traps, wolverines were notoriously named "Indian Devils of the Far North." Bird watchers might catch a glimpse of a bald eagle, an American osprey, or even a yellow-bellied cuckoo. More rare would be a sighting of one of the region's martens, beavers, or fishers, which are in danger of extinction.

One can move quickly from environment to environment, community to community, in the Klamath Mountains. Daytime sightseers from Happy Camp might enjoy driving up to Kelly Lake by way of Indian Creek Road. Take this shady byway on the west side of town and follow it northward. About halfway up to the Gray Back Pass watch for a road on the left and a sign to Kelly Lake. Kelly Lake is clear, aquablue, and deeper than it looks. It is well-stocked with rainbow trout, and a nature trail leads up to it and extends around the lake.

## Red Buttes

Within the great eastward bend of the Siskiyous, and running east to west, are the Red Buttes. Although logging roads and cattle grazing have disfigured the land in places, it is still a beautiful wilderness. The most pristine area in the

Red Buttes is the 90,000 acres of the Applegate Valley, found in southern Oregon.

A variety of trails climb from the banks of the Klamath River into Red Butte country. Thompson Creek Trail, upriver from Happy Camp, flanks the strong-flowing Thompson Creek. The trail crosses a variety of slopes, such as Slater Butte, Fourmile Butte, and Jackson Peak.

Devil's Peak Trail, the easternmost patch, is well-posted and just three-tenths of a mile from Seiad Valley. The trail climbs steadily but is not unpleasantly steep. Ponderosa pine, oak, and madrone, some quite old and gnarly, are thickly scattered throughout the forest here. Other trails include Darkey Creek, Kangaroo Creek, and Portuguese Creek.

The Red Buttes can be scary or even dangerous for the inexperienced mountaineer, for much of it is below 5,000 feet and is therefore "rattlesnake country." One of its peaks is dubbed Rattlesnake Mountain. Mama bears may venture into the lower region when raising their young, since man-nurtured gardens, berries, and other plant foods growing nearby are tempting. Mosquitoes and ticks also frequent the area.

## The Marble Mountain Wilderness Area

The Marble Mountains lie to the southeast of the Siskiyous. This rollicking alpine landscape, established as a national forest in 1953, contains some 213,400 acres of rich natural wilderness. The elevation of the slopes average 7,000 feet.

The terrain of the Marble Mountains is unusual. It appears to have been formed by a powerful earth movement that swirled dozens of slopes together and dropped them down again in a strange confusion. A dominant feature in this terrain is the 700 to 1,000 foot white cap on top of Marble Mountain. Thousands of years ago, when the Marbles were covered by a vast and shallow sea, a peneplain, or flat surface of land, formed on the top of this mountain. Organisms became deposited on it, creating this white cap.

Numerous lakes in glaciated pockets are found throughout this wilderness. The most exotic is Spirit Lake, since the forest surrounding it is dotted by sinkholes where marble bedrock has subsided due to underground waters. Giant salamanders are found in these lakes and the ancient Karuk believed that giant serpents with human faces lived in them and preyed on unwary land creatures.

Fast, foaming streams wind downward from these lakes, plunging over steep and rocky cliffs, forming noisy white cascades and murmuring through deep recesses on the mountains. Here, thick evergreen forests grow next to sheer rock cliffs, making the region dangerous to hikers at times.

The Marbles are thickly forested and have many spectacular and scenic trails. Most lead through forests of white fir, Douglas fir, black oak, and weeping spruce. There is an abundance of wildflowers. Rare wildlife, such as bald eagles, ring-tailed cats, and marmots live in these mountains. Native Roosevelt elk have been reintroduced.

Sightseers wishing to visit the Marbles can enter them at various locations, such as Somes Bar, Happy Camp, Seiad Valley, and the Forks of the Salmon. Elk Creek Road, at the south end of Happy Camp, leads along a valley toward these mountains, coming to within four miles of the wilderness area. Bear Creek, Lick Creek, and Elk Creek trails are all found at the top of this road. Wooley Creek Trail, on the Salmon River, is probably the most popular path leading into the Marble Mountains. One mile past Oak Bottom Campground, a sign on the roadside reads: "Trail 7E13, 5 miles." This is the trailhead. Many of the trees near here are uprooted and burned, for a large fire blazed here some time ago. The trail is rocky and switchbacks lead up the side of the mountain to the ridge. The cascading, foamy waters of the Salmon can be seen below.

## The Salmon-Trinity Alps

Most Karuk villages during prehistoric times were located near the confluence of the Klamath and Salmon rivers, between the high Siskiyous and the Marbles. The Salmon-Trinity Alps are found to the south and east of this country. They flank much of the Salmon River and intermingle with the Marble Mountains. The Pacific Crest Trail leads through them.

The Alps extend over 225,000 acres, consisting of some of the most rugged terrain in northern California. Talus, huge boulders, and steep, jagged peaks can be seen above the timber line. Massive granite ridges soar from an alpine landscape.

In the Trinity Alps, there is glaciation east of Thompson Peak (elevation 8,936 feet). Four of the thirty or so glaciers discovered in the Klamath Mountains exist in the Trinity Alps. Small streams plunge down the mountain crests of these Alps from dozens of native lakes filled with trout. Many of these lakes form the headwaters of large streams, such as the Shasta River which journeys through the Shasta Valley east of the Klamath Mountains.

## Six Rivers National Forest

Most of Karuk country is located in the Klamath Mountains. However, landscape surrounding Orleans is presumably part of the Six Rivers National Forest in Humboldt County, so it will be mentioned briefly.

The elevation of this forest ranges from 500 to 7,000 feet. The northern part is mountainous and much of it is considered sacred country to the Northwestern California Indians. Green hills and meadows, to the south, are sprinkled with flowers in the spring and sparkle with snow in the winter.

The whole mountainous region of northwestern California is a nature lover's paradise. Fortunate sightseers might catch a glimpse of a bald eagle or a blue heron snatching a fat salmon from the Klamath, an elk loping across a meadow in the Marbles, or a mountain lion slinking through the tall, sweeping grass in search of a mouse. An abundance of wild grapes, blackberries, and black raspberries growing along streams and creeks are ready for harvest from late August to early October. It would take several chapters to record a decent list of the flowering plants and trees found within the region.

## Endnotes

1. William L. Bright, *Karok* in *Handbook of North American Indians*, R. F. Heizer, ed., vol. 8, p. 188.

2. Ibid., p. 180.

3. A. L. Kroeber, *Handbook of the Indians of California*, p. 100.

4. Ibid., p. 99.

5. Towns adapted from A. L. Kroeber, *Karok Towns*, University of California Publications in American Archaeology and Ethnology, vol. 35, no. 4; Edward S. Curtis, *The North American Indian*, vol. 13; William L. Bright, *The Karok Language*; and Gary B. Palmer, *Karok World Renewal and Village Sites*.

6. Stanley J. Balfrey, *History of the Schools in Siskiyou County*, p. 126.

7. Ibid., p. 54.

8. Scenic information on the mountains of Karuk territory is derived in part from John Hart, *Hiking the Bigfoot Country: Exploring the Wildlands of Northern California and Southern Oregon* and S. Hawkins and D. Bleything, *Getting Off on Ninety-Six and Other Less Traveled Roads*.

9. A. L. Kroeber and Edward W. Gifford, *World Renewal: A Cult System of Native Northwest California*, University of California Anthropological Records, vol. 13, no. 1, p. 21.

# Chapter 3

# EVERYDAY LIFE

Kroeber claimed that ninety-five percent of the cultural characteristics pertaining to the Hupa and Yurok also pertained to the Karuk.[1] Although all three possessed elements of the California heartland culture existing to the south and east of them, they were primarily members of the great Northwest Pacific Coast Culture centered in British Columbia. Anthropologists label their unique lifestyle the Northwestern California Culture. This chapter describes the everyday material life of the Karuk as it was when the earliest migrants began to enter into the Klamath River country in the early 1850s.

## Physical Features

The Karuk have been characterized by outsiders as slender, strong and muscular with medium statures and small hands and feet. Their skin coloration is light bronze or cinnamon and their eyes are large and have an almond contour. Square or oval-shaped faces are highlighted by high cheekbones and straight or Roman-curved noses. Their mouths are firm and their chins are oval shaped and not prominent. Their coarse, dark hair is usually straight while facial and body hair is scanty.[2]

Both men and women wore long hair. Women parted their hair in the middle and tied each side with strips of buckskin so that it would fall in front of their shoulders. Men wore their hair in a single roll down the back or tied up at the nape.[3] When in mourning, both sexes burned their hair off to a uniform length of one inch.

When girls came of age, they went through traditional menstrual ceremonies which symbolized their entry into

27

*Photo 3. Karuk dwelling house showing the entrance. Siskiyou County Museum.*

*Photo 4. Karuk sweathouse at Orleans. Left to right: P. L. Young, Sandy Bar Joe, Jim Davis, and Webb. Humboldt State University Library.*

On ceremonial occasions the Upriver People decorated their garments with strings of shells, pine nuts, or bear-lily braids. Women wore shell necklaces and men wore headbands enhanced with woodpecker scalps and other feathers.

# Houses[6]

Everyday houses were of three kinds: the family dwelling house, the menstrual hut, and the sweathouse. They were constructed from cedar boards and remained quite warm and comfortable in the winter. During the fall, families camped in temporary huts of fir bark in order to gather acorns from the oak groves. These camps were called *ikveeshrihraam*.

The dwelling house (*ikrivraam*) was a rectangular structure, approximately sixteen by twenty feet, made of roughhewn cedar planks with a stone-laid porch outside. The walls were usually four feet high at the eaves and six feet high at the peak of the roof, which was normally supported by two ridgepoles. In the upriver position of the structure was the door, a two foot wide oval hole low enough to crawl through. The family descended a cedar plank ladder on the inside to a dug out area in the center of the house. The subterranean area was about half the diameter of the interior floor space and two to five feet deep. Here the women and children slept and carried on their family activities. The pit was lined with thin, even and smoothed slabs of wood, and in the center of the pit was a stone-lined fireplace. An opening in the roof above the fireplace served as both a window to admit light and as a flue for the smoke to escape. The family, including the men, ate meals together by the fireplace or in front of the dwelling house. The "shelf" area served for storage of meat, dried fish, and other items in huge storage baskets. It was rarely used to sleep on.

Women used the menstrual hut monthly, or as needed, because of the many taboos associated with their female functions. This hut was a small, rectangular structure built of vertically inclined cedar slabs.

Men and boys used the sweathouse (*ikmaháchraam*) as a clubhouse for conversing and gambling with each other, and as a sleeping area. Admittance was determined by ownership, kinship, or friendship. Entrance of the sweathouse was prohibited to women, except during the initiation of the female shaman. In the words of Powers: No woman "may enter the assembly chamber on penalty of death."[7] Sweathouses were smaller than dwelling houses, but they were built much the same. Their firepits were more elaborate, and only one ridgepole supported the roof planks. Instead of one door, the sweathouse had two doors, one for entry and one for exit. The sweathouse had no shelf, the entire floor area being excavated and covered with well-smoothed cedar planks or large slabs of stone, which were kept swept clean. Carved wooden blocks served as pillows for the men when sleeping.

In winter, fires were built in the sweathouse each morning and evening. The collecting of firewood by men for the sweathouse was considered a sacred duty. Branches had to be cut from the uphill or downhill sides of full-grown fir trees, while accompanied by weeping and prayers for success in hunting and gambling. After gathering the wood, the collector would enter the sweathouse, build a fire, and sweat with the rest of the men. When thoroughly heated, all the men would rush to the river to jump in and cool off.[8] Sweating was accomplished by dry heat, not steaming, which was unknown to the Indians of northwestern California.

## Subsistence

The Upriver People lived bountiful lives as fishermen and foragers. They were fortunate, for more species of flora and fauna existed within their range than anywhere else in California.[9] They fished in the rivers and creeks, hunted wild game in the fir forests and mountain slopes, and gathered wild plant foods from the hillsides. Tobacco was the only plant they cultivated.[10]

Fish served as the main food source, besides acorns (*xuntápan*). Although many species of fish swam in the streams, salmon (*áama*) and steelhead were considered the most important. A ceremony was held each spring to commemorate the gift of new salmon that journeyed up the Klamath from the Pacific Ocean each year to spawn.

Mass fishing, or the taking of fish continuously without moving to a new location, was the usual method. A few days of this could provide a whole winter's fish supply. The Karuk used weirs and a variety of nets and traps to mass fish.[11]

Karuk men also caught fish, mainly for sport, by noosing or riding sturgeon, jerking trout, or shooting salmon with bows and arrows. Other methods included harpooning with spears that had detachable points and fishing with multiple-hooked lines set on poles.[12] The Karuk caught lampreys on warm spring nights.

Children and older people sometimes ate freshwater crayfish (*xanthuun*). They used a lifting net (*imvarum*) to capture them or a pole and string baited with salmon gills. The lifting net consisted of a large openwork, plate-formed basket with a four-foot stick attached to its center. The stick enabled it to remain horizontal when lowered into a still place in the river. Salmon gills were set on the basket as bait. After the crayfish crawled onto the net, it was quickly lifted. Children strung the shells of the crayfish together and used them as toys.[13]

The Karuk consumed more seafood than they did freshwater crayfish, but the amount of seafood consumed overall was not great. They obtained ocean mussels, clams, and saltwater crabs by trading with the Yurok and by visiting the coast themselves. The most important ocean mussel to the Indians of northwestern California was the large *Mytilus californianus*, which the Karuk called *axthah*. It grows up to nine inches long and lives on rocks exposed to the tide. Abalone was also brought over from the coast on rare occasions. As it was difficult to cut, it was seldom eaten. The shells had more value to the Karuk than the meat.[14]

*Photo 5. Karuk man fishing with a dip net on the Klamath River. Siskiyou County Museum.*

Surf fish and seaweed (*xêem*) were obtained from the coast as well. These items furnished salt, needed for good health. The Karuk gathered and dried edible seaweed wherever the shore was rocky. It was used as a food and condiment in most households, while only wealthy families consumed the rarer surf fish.[15]

The Upriver People considered deer (*púufich*) the most prized game, especially the albino deer, whose skin was highly valued during ceremonies. Sweating, bathing, scarification and bleeding for luck, fasting, and sexual continence were all means by which the hunter prepared himself for the hunt. Besides this, the hunter purified his weapons with herbal smoke.

Hunters donned deerhead masks and pretended to graze quietly like deer themselves in order to sneak up on them. Elk and deer were sometimes herded with dogs into ravines and trapped, or run into noose snares set on trails. Some of these snaring locations were privately owned.

After the kill, mainly by the use of bows and arrows, men butchered the animal in the forest and carried it home in a bundle. The Karuk believed that deer were reborn after they were eaten.

Bear (*vírusur*) were usually hunted by the Karuk in the winter. The hunters would find a cave with a hibernating bear in it and attempt to lure it out. If it did not come out on its own, a group of men would drag it out, and then kill it.

Other wild game that served as important food items included small mammals, rodents, and some birds. The Karuk prized the red-headed woodpecker, for they used its feathers during ceremonies.

Wild game not eaten included all canines, wild cats, amphibians, and most insects, as well as gophers, moles, and bats. Such birds as eagles, hawks, owls, meadowlarks, bluejays, crows, ravens, and vultures also were not consumed. Eating bear meat and salmon together was a taboo.[16]

The Upriver People knew of the uses for several hundred species of plants. While most were made into medicines and other necessities, such as baskets and dyes, a large number were used as a food or beverage.[17] These included seeds from various grasses, which the Karuk parched with coals in a basket, and other plants, such as tarweed, and various kinds of berries, grapes, and other fruits. Nuts, such as pine nuts and hazel nuts, were also eaten, as well as various bulbs and greens.[18]

Acorns were the major plant food, although their bitter tannic acid had to be removed before they were edible. This was done by cracking and drying the acorns, rubbing them to remove the skins and then grinding them to flour with a stone pestle and slab. The flour was then sifted and leached in a sand pit to remove the poison.[19] The most popular type of acorn came from the tanbark oak. Black oak, live oak, and post oak are other types of acorn-bearing trees growing in Karuk country.

## Preparing Food

The Karuk normally cooked fresh fish and meat by roasting either one over a fire of hot coals. They also could be dried on a scaffold and preserved for later use. An earth oven of hot stones with a fire built on top was sometimes used to cook meat and edible plant bulbs.[20]

The preparation of fish depended upon its use.[21] The Karuk cured and stored most fish for the winter. Dried steelhead, because of its higher fat content, molded more easily than salmon, so the Karuk ate it first, while dried salmon lasted throughout the year when properly stored. During the salmon season fresh salmon was roasted on skewer sticks at the fire, cut into smaller pieces, and then eaten.

The Karuk sun-dried smaller species of fish. In the early morning, or when fog intervened, this drying was aided by the use of small fires smoldering under low, open racks.

*Photo 6. Karuk woman preparing acorn meal at Ka'tim'iin. Siskiyou County Museum.*

Later in the day the sun's rays were usually sufficient to cure the fish.

After catching the salmon, the Karuk cured those to be prepared for winter storage as quickly as possible. First the tail of the salmon was cut off to drain the blood. Then, after removing the head, the salmon was cut full length up the belly and its backbone removed. This left two large slabs of salmon flesh, which could then be spitted on sticks of willow or poison oak and placed on scaffolds above a small fire to be dried and smoked. Steatite bowls caught the grease. Usually after a preliminary drying of a few days in the small lean-to smoke hut, women hung the salmon steaks on regular drying racks in the dwelling house. After a total of eight to ten days of curing the slabs were ready to be stored.

The backbone of the salmon was sometimes dried and used as dog food during the winter months. Salmon eggs were always saved and hung on sticks outside to be sun-dried. They could be eaten or pulverized. No one cared to eat them fresh, as there was such an abundance of food during the fishing season.

Karuk women used two methods to store salmon. Some-times they used the same large storage baskets that were used for storing acorns. But the fish did not keep all winter in this manner. In warm weather, the fish became rancid and subject to the ravages of insects. Caches at the back of the dwelling house served as the preferred method of storing salmon. Women lined the pit with pine needles, sometimes mixed with maple leaves, laid the fish inside and covered it with more pine needles. Caches kept the flavor better than storage baskets and the fish were less likely to be attacked by insects or become moldy.

Venison and other meats were also smoked. Women col-lected rotten wood from alder, madrone, oak, and certain other trees for this curing process. Sometimes they dipped the wood in water to make it burn slower and to produce more smoke. Dead, dry limbs were preferred because they broke easily when hit on the ground.

After the bitter tannic acid had been removed from the acorn flour in the sand pit, the resulting acorn dough was mixed with water and boiled in a large water-resilient basket to make acorn soup or mush (xuun). To make bread, the dough was cooked on hot stones.[22]

Karuk women broke off the dried leaves of edible seaweed and crushed them into flakes to use as a condiment with acorn soup. Wealthier women laid one or two surf fish on a small openwork tray at the top of the acorn gruel.

Sometimes women buried acorns in the muddy sand to soak for a year or more and then boiled them with the hull still on. They could then be cracked with the teeth and eaten.[23]

The Karuk ate other plants as is, crushed them with stone pestles in mortars, dried them in the sun, or prepared and cooked them in a basket of twine weave, like acorns. Plants were also made into teas and juices.

Many tribes in California used the juice of the milkweed (*Asclepias*) for chewing gum. They dropped the thick milky fluid into a basket of boiling water where it soon floated on the top as a rubberlike substance which could be chewed. The Karuk called this gum *imshaxvuh*.[24]

## Production

Everything the Karuk needed or used in their secular and religious lives existed within their territorial limits or could easily be obtained through trade. The Upriver People continually foraged the countryside for food, firewood, and raw materials, and participated in an elaborate trade network with their neighbors.

The materials used by the Karuk came strictly from the earth. They created baskets, ropes, and medicines with plants and their fibers. Blankets and clothing were fashioned with animal hides. Bones, horns, shells, wood, and stones were used to create other implements.

Plant fibers served many purposes. With them, women made some of the most beautiful baskets in North America. The long, sword-shaped leaves of the *Iris macrosiphon* (Karuk: *ápkaas*), found throughout the countryside, were gathered and two thin, tough but silky fibers scraped from each leaf. These fibers were then twisted into cords and woven into fishing nets and bags, and used to make rope.[25] Although twisting was a tedious task, the procedure resulted in an unusually fine, hard, and even string. Grapevine served as a convenient tying material when the special pliability of ropes or strings was not needed.

Shamans and doctors used a variety of plants for curing purposes. Tobacco (*ihêeraha*) was the only plant that the Karuk cultivated. Besides being used to sooth patients or for pleasure smoking, it was used as an offering to the Ikxaréeyav during religious and ceremonial events. Hunters made the same kind of offering before engaging in a hunt.

Men smoked it at bedtime in the sweathouse.[26] Pungent and powerful, it quickly produced dizziness and sleep. The Karuk avoided harvesting wild tobacco because of the fear that it may have sprung up from a grave. Other medicinal plants utilized by the Karuk include mistletoe, ginger root, milkweed, mint, and lace fern.[27]

Animal skins were sewn into a variety of needed items, especially blankets and clothing. Karuk men fashioned elkhide or rods of wood into armor for times of battle. Quivers for carrying arrows were made from the skins of smaller animals.[28] Feathers and scalps of birds and rodents were used during ceremonies. Deerhoof and cocoon rattles served as musical instruments.

The skin of the sturgeon or salmon was chewed, then boiled and mixed with the pitch of the young Douglas fir and the gum of wild plum, or chokecherry, to make glue.[29] The Karuk prepared it as needed in small stone dishes. Any leftover remained in the dish to be used again, and was later softened with a few drops of water. Pigments added to the glue produced paints for decorating bows, arrows, and certain other implements.

Shell was fashioned into spoons and used as ornaments during ceremonies. Awls and fish-hooks were made of bone. From horn was fashioned ornate spoons, purses, and cutting and splitting wedges. Elk-horn wedges were used to split wood and stone adzes to smooth it.[30]

The Karuk used wood for many different purposes. They split wooden planks from cedar logs to build their structures. Bows were made of yew wood, with a sinew backing and a sinew bowstring, while arrows were fashioned from syringa wood.[31] Other wooden implements included highly decorated treasure chests, storage boxes, seats, and head-rests for men; utensils such as cooking paddles, spoons, and meat platters; and musical instruments such as whistles, flutes, and rattles.[32]

Wealthy men obtained redwood canoes (*paah*), an excellent means of long distance river travel, from the coastal

*Photo 7. Old woman carrying firewood in a burden basket. Humboldt State University Library.*

Yurok.[33] Built from half of a redwood log, these canoes were square-ended, round-bottomed, and heavy. They were nicely finished with recurved gunwales and carved-out seats. Although varying considerably in breadth and beam, the standard length of these redwood canoes was eighteen feet. Long, stout paddles served as both pole and oar.[34]

The Karuk used stones daily. They placed them on hearths and in cooking baskets, and used them as grinding slabs and pestles. Other stones served for mauls and adzes, or for arrow points and knife blades. Because stones were so often utilized, the Upriver People could quickly identify their physical properties, such as texture, hardness, cleavage, and color.[35]

Steatite, or soapstone, cracked less easily than other rocks when heated and was soft to carve.[36] From it the Karuk carved pipe bowls and dishes for catching salmon grease. Shamans and some priests fashioned tubular pipes entirely with this stone. These six-inch pipes were used often during religious events.[37]

*Photo 8. Fritz Hansen straightening an arrow. Smithsonian Institution.*

*Photo 9. Karuk man standing in a canoe, paddling or poling. Smithsonian Institution.*

Men flaked obsidian into ceremonial blades, everyday knives, arrowheads, and other treasured tools. Because obsidian is brittle and glassy, it was easily shaped into thin, sharp blades, making it more valuable than other stones used for such purposes. Red obsidian, because of its rarity, was the most valuable of all.

## Trade

A well-established trade network existed among the Indians of the Pacific Coast. The wealth and trade items supplied by each group was determined by the favorability of their immediate environment. The Karuk, wealthy for California Indians, traded mainly among their nearest neighbors and among themselves, although they sometimes went on trading expeditions to the coast or other places.

The Upriver People obtained many items through trade and traded many items themselves. They supplied shells, seaweed, baskets, tobacco seeds, salt, tan oak acorns, and canoes to the upriver Shasta, and acquired, in turn, from them black or cloudy red obsidian blades, deerskins, wolfskins, sugar pine nuts, juniper beads, and basketry caps.[38] From the Yurok, they obtained redwood canoes, pipes, salt, seashells, and bows painted red and blue.[39] Dentalium shells and baskets were also traded to the Konomihu, who lived around the Forks of Salmon, in exchange for furs and deerskin clothing.[40] Sometimes the Karuk used money, that is dentalium shells, to obtain the goods they needed.

## Endnotes

1. A. L. Kroeber, *Handbook of the Indians of California*, p. 98.

2. Theodora Kroeber and R. F. Heizer, *Almost Ancestors: The First Californians*, p. 51.

3. William L. Bright, *Karok* in *Handbook of North American Indians*, R. F. Heizer, ed., vol. 8, p. 184.

4. William L. Bright, *The Karok Language*, p. 301.

5. Information on clothing is adapted primarily from William L. Bright, *Karok* in *Handbook of North American Indians*, R. F. Heizer, ed., vol. 8, p. 184.

6. Information on houses is adapted from William L. Bright, *Karok* in *Handbook of North American Indians*, R. F. Heizer, ed., vol. 8, pp. 182-184; Edward S. Curtis, *The North American Indian*, vol. 13, p. 217; and A. L. Kroeber, *Handbook of the Indians of California*, pp. 78-82, unless otherwise noted.

7. Stephen Powers, *Tribes of California*, p. 24.

8. Ibid., p. 25 and William L. Bright, *Karok* in *Handbook of North American Indians*, R. F. Heizer, ed., vol. 8, p. 183.

9. David W. Lantis, et al, *California: Land of Contrast*, p. 387.

10. John P. Harrington, *Tobacco Among the Karuk Indians of California*.

11. A. L. Kroeber and S. A. Barrett, *Fishing Among the Indians of Northwestern California*, University of California Anthropological Records, vol. 21, nos. 1-2, p. 8.

12. Ibid. and William L. Bright, *Karok* in *Handbook of North American Indians*, R. F. Heizer, ed., vol. 8, p. 181.

13. A. L. Kroeber and S. A. Barrett, *Fishing Among the Indians of Northwestern California*, University of California Anthropological Records, vol. 21, nos. 1-2, p. 114.

14. Ibid, pp. 110-112.

15. Ibid., p. 110.

16. Information on wild game and Karuk hunting practices comes primarily from William L. Bright, *Karok* in *Handbook of North American Indians*, R. F. Heizer, ed., vol. 8, pp. 181-182.

17.  Sara M. Schenck and E. W. Gifford, *Karok Ethnobotany*, University of California Anthropological Records, vol. 13, no. 6.

18.  William L. Bright, *Karok* in *Handbook of North American Indians*, R. F. Heizer, ed., vol. 8, p. 183.

19.  Ibid., p. 182.

20.  Ibid.

21.  Information on the preparation of fish is adapted primarily from A. L. Kroeber and S. A. Barrett, *Fishing Among the Indians of Northwestern California*, University of California Anthropological Records, vol. 21, nos. 1-2, pp. 99-105.

22.  William L. Bright, *Karok* in *Handbook of North American Indians*, R. F. Heizer, ed., vol. 8, pp. 182-183.

23.  Ibid.

24.  C. Hart Merriam, *Ethnographic Notes on California Indian Tribes, II*, ed. and comp. by R. F. Heizer, Reports of the University of California Archaeological Survey, no. 68, p. 212.

25.  Edward S. Curtis, *The North American Indian*, vol. 13, p. 217.

26.  John P. Harrington, *Tobacco Among the Karuk Indians of California*.

27.  C. Hart Merriam, *Ethnographic Notes on California Indian Tribes, II*, ed. and comp. by R. F. Heizer, Reports of the University of California Archaeological Survey, no. 68, p. 209.

28.  William L. Bright, *Karok* in *Handbook of North American Indians*, R. F. Heizer, ed., vol. 8, p. 183.

29.  John P. Harrington, *Tobacco Among the Karuk Indians of California*, pp. 156-157

30.  Edward S. Curtis, *The North American Indian*, vol. 13, p. 217.

31.  A. L. Kroeber, *Handbook of the Indians of California*, p. 89 and William L. Bright, *Karok* in *Handbook of North American Indians*, R. F. Heizer, ed., vol. 8, p. 183.

32.  A. L. Kroeber, *Handbook of the Indians of California*, pp. 92-96.

33.  Ibid., p. 82.

34.  Ibid., pp. 82-83.

35.  R. F. Heizer and A. E. Treganza, "Mines and Quarries of the Indians of California," *The California Indians: A Source Book*, R. F. Heizer and M. A. Whipple, eds., p. 346.

36.  Ibid., p. 347.

37.  John P. Harrington, *Tobacco Among the Karuk Indians of California*, pp. 150-155.

38.  James T. Davis, *Trade Routes and Economic Exchange Among the Indians of California*, Reports of the University of California Archaeological Survey, no. 54, pp. 24-25.

39.  Ibid. and John P. Harrington, *Tobacco Among the Karuk Indians of California*, pp. 162-163.

40.  James T. Davis, *Trade Routes and Economic Exchange Among the Indians of California*, Reports of the University of California Archaeological Survey, no. 54, pp. 24-25.

*Photo 10. Henry Joseph of Happy Camp holding a Karuk box drum. Siskiyou County Museum.*

# Chapter 4

# THE ARTS

The Karuk had an advanced technology for prehistoric people. Since they survived graciously off the land by fishing and foraging, they had extra time to devote to the development of an elaborate culture. Art, music, games, and mythology were all prevalent aspects of their lives.

Artistic skills were remarkably developed. While women created intricately decorated baskets, men carved wood and horn into ornately fashioned treasure boxes, cooking paddles, and spoons.[1]

Music was important during dances and ceremonies. The Karuk singing style, similar to the Hupa and the Yurok, had a wider range of rhythm, pitch, and intonation than that of other California Indians. The northwesterner, says Kroeber, loved to jump upward an octave or more to a long and powerful note, then fall back from this by a series of slides that were frequently a continuous tonal transition.[2] Instruments, such as rattles, drums, and bone whistles, accompanied the singing. Men also knew how to play their bows and wooden flutes for amusement and for serenading. In more recent times, Karuk men made drums by covering a wooden box with hide. They were beat upon in time to gambling songs in order to bring luck to the players.[3]

Gambling, the most popular recreational activity for men, took place each evening in the sweathouse.[4] The men gambled with a group of small sticks, one marked with a ring around the middle, which were held in two hands and shuffled behind the back. The opponent tried to guess which hand held the marked stick (or ace). Men often bet with dentalium shells or other treasures. Gambling served as an important means of acquiring wealth.

*Photo 11. Karuk flute player (Bernard Jerry). Smithsonian Institution.*

*Photo 12. Hackett using his bow as a musical instrument. Smithsonian Institution.*

The Karuk still gamble, especially after the World Renewal Ceremony. Nowadays the Hupa and Karuk compete with modern money. They throw a blanket on the ground and use the gambling sticks. As they play, the Hupa face upriver, and the Karuk face downriver, possibly for luck. Women may watch, but they are not allowed to participate.

Men also played shinny and still do. This is a stick game similar to hockey.[5] Three-men teams, equipped with heavy sticks, compete by throwing a "tossel," two wooden blocks attached by a buckskin cord, across opposing goal lines. Players try to hinder their opponents by grappling, wrestling, and cudgeling with their playing sticks. Two men serve as referees, one for each team.

Other games played during historic times include cat's cradle, archery, and dart throwing.[6] The Karuk still compete in archery games. They put money in a treasure box and the one who gets closest to the bull's eye wins.

Women played a type of dice game with mussel shells.[7] In 1925, Kroeber observed that beaver teeth dice were attributed to the Karuk in one or two museum collections. But since these teeth are an Oregonian trait, they may have reached the Karuk only since American occupation.[8]

Ceremonies also served as a form of recreation. The regalia worn, songs sung, and the dance steps performed often were competitive, with one village trying to outdo another.

## Oral Literature

Storytelling, besides being recreational, served as a form of education. Karuk mythology, like most indigenous mythology, gave an explanation for the origin of their world and its present features. Myths were used to explain the origin of certain plants, abstractions such as pain or joy, customs, implements, or the reason for the coloring of a bird or for the distinctive characteristics of certain animals. Central to Karuk mythology was a previous race of immortals or spirit beings called the Ikxaréeyav, which included, among others, a culture hero who was both a trickster (usually coyote) and

*Photo 13. Playing the Indian stick game. Siskiyou County Museum.*

a monster-destroyer. As a culture hero, he was responsible for certain things in the world but did not create the world.[9] According to one myth, an immortal named Ikhareyau (probably a different spelling of Ikxaréeyav) appeared at Ka'tim'iin and created the world, afterwards begetting the race of people with a certain woman he found.[10]

The Upriver People and their neighbors, according to Norton, believed in a supreme and loving Creator who wished to guide the people in the ways of life.[11] His relationship to the Ikxaréeyav is not clear. It is possible that they represent God's diverse attributes, as manifested in the world.

Myths told by song were the most important type of narrative. They were usually recited on cold winter evenings around a fire, and were primarily accounts of the deeds and exploits of the Ikxaréeyav. The myths usually concluded with the coming of mankind and the transformation of the Ikxaréeyav into species of animals, plants, special rocks, or disembodied spirits, which they believed to still exist among them.[12] The majority of the Ikxaréeyav were known to the Karuk only by the name of that which they had been transformed into. According to another account, some of the immortals vanished across the Pacific Ocean after organizing the Northwestern California Culture.[13] The Ikxaréeyav established all the customs and rituals of the people, such as those having to do with the acquisition and preparation of food, birth, puberty, marriage, sickness, death, the social and ethical laws, the rituals for the great ceremonies, and the like. Certain locations were honored with a spiritual or supernatural significance because of their association with the creative acts of the Ikxaréeyav. Some myths were regarded as magical formulas. These were transmitted by individuals who claimed them as personal property and used them to acquire wealth, love, and luck.[14]

The Karuk believed the land of the dead (*yumararik*) to be in the sky. Thus they called the Milky Way the Ghost's Road.[15] One of their terms for the spirit of a dead person was *yuma'ara*. The Upriver People had descriptive terms for many things. For example, they regarded the Pleiades (*atayram tuneechas*) as seven little sisters dancing the Flower Dance across the sky.

The Karuk also believed in evil spirits (*apuruwan*). These spirits caused stars to fall and other minor disasters. One of their signs was a "blue devil fire." Two Karuk informants claimed that they once saw a devil fire burning in a field near their home. It looked to them like a bonfire at first, then became elongated, causing the whole field to look as if it were on fire. If the blue fire entered one's body, death was likely to follow, unless a sucking doctor could suck out the evil spirit. They also told about how one could "go deviling" (*apur*) with "a peculiar, round, pinkish stone." By secretly hiding it on or near another person, the new possessor of the stone was made ill and might die.[16] Evil spirits were thought to cause sickness and death.

## The Calendar

The Karuk calendar year (*hárinay*) was based on a thirteen moon system. Ten moons were numbered and three moons had descriptive appellations only. These last three moons were called "thrown away" because they were not numbered.[17] The three unnumbered moons began the year, preceding the sequence of ten numbered moons. The "beginning of the world" was in September, the month of the World Renewal Ceremony, although for the upriver Karuk at Inaam, this took place one moon earlier. Some of the numbered months also had descriptive names. *Kusra* means moon or month. The calendar year was as follows:[18]

1) **Okvakusra.** This means "the moon of the world renewal rite." Inaam people called this month Yarukvakusra, "downriver people's month," because the Pikyavish was held at Panámniik and Ka'tim'iin at this time. It is equivalent to September.

2) **Náaseepkusra.** This month is equated to October.

3) **Pakuhakusra.** This means "the acorn gathering moon." After having resided in temporary huts during the

gathering season, the people returned to their villages when the winter storms set in. This month corresponds with November.

4) **Yīthahan (kusra).** (The First Moon) This month correlates with December, when the new moon sets in the west. It was known as a "bad month," or *kusraxem*, as there was hardly any fresh food available.

5) **Áxakhan.** (The Second Moon) This was also a "bad month," since it occurred during winter when provisions were scarce. It is equivalent to January.

6) **Kuyraakhan.** (The Third Moon) Another cold month, it is loosely equivalent to January and February. The second and third moons were telescoped together, or one was dropped, after the winter solstice had been reached to account for the fact that there are more than twelve but less than thirteen lunations in the solar year.

7) **Piithvâan.** (The Fourth Moon) This is the time of *pitvaraiwa*, "looking about the house in vain for food." Women began digging *tayish*, or Indian potatoes, which have white blossoms. People built fires in the open meadows to keep warm while searching for this first plant food available in the spring. This moon is equivalent to February.

8) **Itrôopaan.** (The Fifth Moon) More types of roots were available for eating during this month. It is equated to March.

9) **Ikrívkihaan.** (The Sixth Moon) Also called Iruravahivkusra, or "the moon of the Spring Salmon Ceremony," this was a time that greens were harvested. The First Salmon Ceremony took place at Ameekyáaraam, and it was sometimes held a moon earlier. This month corresponds with April.

10) **Xakinívkihan.** (The Seventh Moon) This month correlates with May.

11) **Kuyrakinívkihan.** (The Eighth Moon) This month is equivalent to June.

12) **Itroopatíshaamnihan.** (The Ninth Moon) Also called Ahavaríkusra, or "animals in heat moon," the Ameekyáaraam Jump Dance was held at this time. This is the month of July.

13) **Itráyarhan.** (The Tenth Moon) This moon was also known as Karukvakusra, "the moon of the upriver Karuk," because their Pikyavish took place in this month ten days before the moon's waning. This is the month of August.

The Karuk counting system was based upon the numbers five and ten. These numbers had ritual significance.

## Basketry

To the Karuk and to most Native Americans, basketry is a work of art—an art in which hope, aspiration, desire, love, religion, poetry, national pride, and mythology are all interwoven. The Karuk created baskets for both utilitarian and decorative purposes. They used them to preserve, prepare, and cook food, for gathering acorns and other edible items, and even as tokens to end battles.

Girls began weaving as young as six years old.[19] Young girls would practice with one strand or they would watch and copy their older relatives. The older women sometimes helped the young girls. Men never wove baskets, although they did weave fish-nets with twine they made themselves.[20] Karuk basketry, like that of their neighbors, is characterized by circular open baskets, somewhat rounded at the bottom, and generally shallow in depth. Large storage baskets were proportionately deeper.[21]

Karuk women worked hard and traveled far to gather basketry material.[22] This chore, besides the preparation of the fibers, was no easy task. All the processes of gathering, preparing, sorting, and storing of materials the Karuk women described as "make." Every woman who was able prepared her own material. However, small children in the home, physical disability, or extreme old age were legitimate reasons for not going after the available materials.[23]

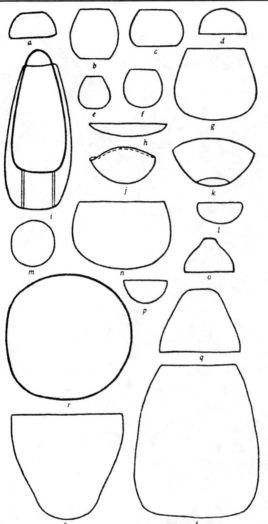

**Fig. 2.** Traditional shapes and proportions of Yurok-Karok baskets. **a,** dress cap; **b,** fancy basket; **c,** fancy basket; **d,** work cap; **e,** tobacco basket; **f,** spoon basket; **g,** water basket; **h,** Indian plate; **i,** cradle; **j,** cap used by Karok men for tobacco container; **k,** hopper; **l,** soup basket; **m,** sifter; **n,** cooking basket; **o,** cover; **p,** dipper; **q,** cover for large basket or old fashioned seed basket (now used for gathering materials used in Brush dance); **r,** mealing tray; **s,** wood packing basket; **t,** storage basket. Reproduced from Lila M. O'Neale *Yurok-Karok Basket Weavers,* University of California Publications in American Archaeology and Ethnology, vol. 32, no. 1 (1932)

*Photo 14. Woman (Phoebe Maddox ?) making baskets; baby in cradleboard. Smithsonian Institution.*

The only way a woman could tell whether a basket had been made by her people was by the material and the design used. This generally reflected the time-honored basketmaking traditions of the tribe, which, according to Kroeber, were virtually identical among the Karuk, Yurok, and Hupa. The Karuk had a large supply of plant materials to choose from in their native region, but the woodwardia fern, which they always dyed red, was characteristically their favorite for decorative purposes. Additionally, they were more inclined to use patterns containing vertical outlines in their basketry.[24]

Since the Shasta had fewer plant fibers to choose from than the Klamath River Indians, the Karuk often traded baskets to them. Shasta women did manufacture their own baskets, although rarely, depending more upon trade with the Karuk. These resembled Karuk and Yurok baskets of poorer finish, and typically showed a simple pattern of vertical bars.[25]

Twining was the only weaving method followed by the Indians of northwestern California, although coiled weaves were used incidentally as a border finish.[26] The twining technique required braiding the strands around a warp rib, with each strand covering one side of the rib.

Three separate categories of materials were used: foundation materials, twining elements, and overlay materials.[27] The foundation materials were used to make frames and handles. The fibrous twining elements provided strength to the weaving, and the overlay materials sealed the basket and created decorative patterns.

Foundation materials included hazel sticks (asip), willow sticks, myrtle sticks, and wild lilac shoots. Women collected the wild lilac shoots in June or July and used them only for very small baskets. Hazel sticks, used in large handled baskets and dress hats, were gathered in the spring from an area that had been burned a year or two previously. The foundation materials were peeled immediately, when still fresh and green, and then dried.[28]

Twining elements included tree roots, such as yellow pine, bull or pitch pine, sugar pine, alder, wild grape, and cottonwood. The small roots became exposed after winter flood waters receded. They were normally gathered in December, January, and February.[29] Roots were dug from beneath the earth, cut a short distance from the trunk, and then roasted.

To roast the roots, women made a fire on the sand and then buried the roots underneath in the hot sand. After roasting for a sufficient period of time, the roots were taken out of the sand and the bark peeled off while still hot. The women split the roots into thin strips and dried them. To make them pliable, the strips were soaked and then scraped with a sharp instrument so that the tough fibers could be pulled from the strips.[30] The roots made up the interior of the basket.

Overlay materials included white or snake grass, woodwardia fern, maidenhair fern, and porcupine quills. Karuk women gathered these plants between June and September, except for the woodwardia fern, which could be gathered anytime except in the spring. Quills were gathered anytime one found a dead porcupine or killed one.[31]

Karuk women found woodwardia fern (*tiip tiip*) in moist, shady places. After pulling off the feathery leaves, the long stems were crushed and two long strings, the length of the stalk, were removed. These strings were then dried. Later they were dyed red with a solution made from the bark of an old alder tree. To make the dye, the alder bark was broken into small pieces and pulverized, then placed in a large pan and covered with water. After being dyed, the strands were taken out to be dried.[32]

Karuk women obtained white grass from an area that had been burned a year or two previously. The long center shoots were gathered and laid out in the sun to blacken and dry. They were turned over several times a day and brought in at night. After drying the grass, the women stored it in a cool place.[33]

The maidenhair fern provided the black pattern found in Karuk baskets. Good stock grows high up in rocky creek beds that are difficult to reach. The black sides of the stems were peeled off from the reddish undersides by running the stems through a split in a straight-grained piece of wood.[34] Before use, the amount needed for a basket was soaked in water to make it pliable.

Porcupine quills were the most difficult with which to weave. After dyeing them yellow with either wild parsnip or high-altitude moss, which is a deep yellow, the quills were boiled and rinsed in cold water and left to dry. The women snipped off the sharp ends on both sides and flattened the quill as much as possible so it would be easier and more flexible to work with.[35]

The work always began with the foundation materials and the twining elements. Weaving began at the bottom of the frame. Fibers of the bull pine roots, for example, were frequently used to start the forming of the basket bottom. As the twining progressed, each foundation stick or shoot would be woven securely into position and the shape of the basket would appear.[36] Lastly, women worked in the overlay materials, creating beautiful designs with them.

Karuk weavers decided upon their own designs and materials when creating baskets. Although the motifs they selected had been handed down for generations, each basket was a unique work of art. Artists and historians alike greatly admire the excellence and durability of these baskets.

## Types of Baskets

The Karuk made baskets for many different purposes. The following is a list of some of the kinds used by them:

**Basketry Caps.** Both men and women wore basketry caps (*ápxaan*). Men's caps were deeper in cut than the women's. They used two types: the common everyday hat, which was coarsely woven and lightly lined, and the dress-up hat, which was highly decorated and overlaid with bear grass.[37]

**Tobacco Baskets.** These baskets, called *iheerahasipnuuk*, were always semi-circular in form. The opening at its top or mouth was closed by buckskin held in place with a thong. Vertical and diagonal patterns were its only designs. Sometimes, an old hat with a slit at one side served as a tobacco pouch.[38]

**Money Baskets.** These baskets looked similar to tobacco pouches except that their patterns were larger. The Karuk kept woodpecker rolls, dentalium strings, and other small treasures in them.[39]

**Trays.** The tray (*muruk*) had many uses. A close-twined variety, about eighteen inches across, was used exclusively to serve deer meat. Another, more open-twined, variety, as large as thirty inches in diameter, served to dry fish, fruit, or acorns over the fire, and as a sifter to winnow beans. Trays were made of hazel or willow sticks and were typically left undecorated.[40]

**Cooking Baskets.** These large cookers, called *tharámpuukrav*, ranged in width from one to three feet. They were woven so tightly that acorn soup could be made in them. The Karuk made them with hazel or willow sticks, root twining elements, and with white grass overlay patterns.[41]

**Soup Bowls.** Made just like the larger cooking baskets, the Upriver People used these smaller serving baskets (*pátarav*) to serve acorn soup of any variety. One Karuk woman keeps such a bowl in her cupboard along with her modern dishes.

**Burden Baskets.** Burden baskets (*átimnam*) were made large or small, depending on the use. Large, open-twined varieties were used to carry wood or other supplies, such as the equipment needed to make acorn soup. Each had a special strap that encircled the forehead when being carried.

**Storage Baskets.** Storage baskets in general were called *sipnuuk*. Some of these closely woven containers were as tall as the weaver's head. They were used to store all manner of things, from fish and cracked acorns to a wealthy man's supply of shell money, woodpecker crests, obsidian blades, and trinkets. A conical basket with the same pattern as the storage basket was sometimes used as a lid.[42]

**Cradles.** Karuk women handcrafted cradles (*tháxtuuy*) with hazel sticks. Their edges were bound with willow or hazel bark, or sometimes the generally discarded red side of the maidenhair fern. Comparatively few Karuk women make cradles today. In former days, one woman usually made them for everyone in her community. This task was immense, since each child needed three or four during the first two years of life.[43]

Women carried the cradles on their backs when taking journeys, tying the baby securely in place with leather straps. Bright says that the infant sat on the strands closing off the foot of the basket, while its feet hung free.[44] When not being carried, the cradle could be hung from its top or propped up at a desired angle.

## Basketry Designs[45]

Karuk basketry designs were very similar to Hupa and Yurok designs. Not every design was appropriate to every kind of basket. For example, cooking or serving baskets tended to have plain designs because patterns which do not require frequent breaking of the overlay material are more likely to remain watertight. Women prided themselves on keeping to their traditional motifs, which have changed little since ancient times. Shown below are examples of design elements frequently used. These elements were often combined with one another to form more intricate patterns. The first illustration to the left in each of the figures below is a simple example of the design element, followed by more complex adaptations.

**Figure 3.** The Karuk *tata'ktak* design, meaning "points," is very common, and is frequently found in combination with other designs. Patterns with rows of notches or points are so named.

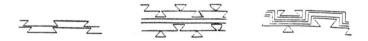

**Figure 4.** Another common Karuk design is called *nutiháníich*, or flintlike. Its basic element is the parallelogram.

**Figure 5.** This Karuk design is called *apsunyufiv*, or snakenose. Kroeber says that the species of snake denoted by *apsun* is not known. The primary element of this design seems to be the isosceles triangle.

**Figure 6.** The *ápxaankuykuy* design is common on basketry caps. The prefix *ápxaan* means basketry cap. *Kuykuy* means up and down, back and forth, or the successive placing of one thing against another.

**Figure 7.** This design is called *ikurukur*, meaning stirred, and may be a way of denoting the spatial zigzag.

**Figure 8.** The Karuk crow-foot design, *anaachfithi*, has as its distinguishing element a right-angled triangle at the end of a bar or stem. It is more common on Yurok baskets. There is a considerable amount of variation in this pattern.

**Figure 9.** The Karuk *xurip*, or straight bar design, is shown here.

**Figure 10.** This Karuk pattern is called *en i'kiviti*, or cut wood. The characteristic feature is the steplike effect, which gives this pattern its name.

**Figure 11.** Called *xasi'ree* by the Karuk, this pattern is similar to the ikurukur design. Kroeber states that, contrary to the usual zigzag design, when xasi'ree constitutes a separate zigzag band it appears to be composed of broken lines, and when it follows an outline of triangles, it is detached from them a little distance. Thus, it has a broken or openwork effect.

**Figure 12.** The Karuk design *vakaixara*, long worm, is frequently associated with the flintlike design.

**Figure 13.** *Kixtapis*, frog hand, is a common Karuk hand design.

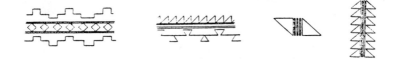

**Figure 14.** Combinations of design elements are shown as follows from left to right: en i'kiviti and apsunyufiv, ápxaankuykuy and tata'ktak, xurip and tata'ktak, xurip and tata'ktak.

## Endnotes

1. A. L. Kroeber, *Handbook of the Indians of California*, pp. 92-94.

2. Ibid., pp. 95-96.

3. Ibid., p. 96.

4. William L. Bright, *Karok* in *Handbook of North American Indians*, R. F. Heizer, ed., vol. 8, p. 183.

5. Ibid., p. 187.

6. Ibid.

7. Ibid.

8. A. L. Kroeber, *Handbook of the Indians of California*, p. 108.

9. A. L. Kroeber, *Types of Indian Culture in California*, University of California Publications in American Archaeology and Ethnology, vol. 2, no. 3, pp. 95-96.

10. Edward S. Curtis, *The North American Indian*, vol. 13, p. 64.

11. Jack Norton, *Genocide in Northwestern California*, p. 3.

12. William L. Bright, *Karok* in *Handbook of North American Indians*, R. F. Heizer, ed., vol. 8, p. 187; Gary Palmer, *Karok World Renewal and Village Sites*, p. 20; and John P. Harrington, *Tobacco Among the Karuk Indians of California*, p. 8.

13. A. L. Kroeber, *Types of Indian Culture in California*, University of California Publications in American Archaeology and Ethnology, vol. 2, no. 3, p. 96.

14. William L. Bright, *Karok* in *Handbook of North American Indians*, R. F. Heizer, ed., vol. 8, p. 187.

15. Ibid., p. 188.

16. Mary E. Arnold and Mabel Reed, *In the Land of the Grasshopper Song*, p. 71.

17. A. L. Kroeber and E. W. Gifford, *World Renewal: A Cult System of Native Northwestern California*, University of California Anthropological Records, vol. 13, no. 1, p. 9.

18. The calendar is adapted from John P. Harrington, *Tobacco Among the Karuk Indians of California*, pp. 82-83 and with reference to A. L. Kroeber and E. W. Gifford, *World Renewal: A Cult System of Native Northwestern California*, University of California Anthropological Records, vol. 13, no. 1, pp. 8-9, 130-131.

19. Lottie Beck, "Karok Basketry," *Siskiyou Pioneer and Yearbook*, vol 4, no. 4, p. 22.

20. Ibid.

21. A. L. Kroeber, *Basket Designs of the Indians of Northwestern California*, University of California Publications in American Archaeology and Ethnology, vol. 2, no. 3, p. 106.

22. Hazel Davis, "The Karok Indians," *Siskiyou Pioneer and Yearbook*, vol. 4, no. 4, p. 6.

23. Lila M. O'Neale, *Yurok-Karok Basket Weavers*, University of California Publications in American Archaeology and Ethnology, vol. 32, no. 1, p. 13.

24. A. L. Kroeber, *Basket Designs of the Indians of Northwestern California*, University of California Publications in American Archaeology and Ethnology, vol. 2, no. 3, pp. 116-117.

25. Ibid., p. 149.

26. Ibid., p. 109.

27. Lila M. O'Neale, *Yurok-Karok Basket Weavers*, University of California Publications in American Archaeology and Ethnology, vol. 32, no. 1, p. 14.

28. Hazel Davis, "The Karok Indians," *Siskiyou Pioneer and Yearbook*, vol. 4, no. 4, p. 17.

29. Lottie Beck, "Karok Basketry," *Siskiyou Pioneer and Yearbook*, vol. 4, no. 4, p. 22.

30. Hazel Davis, "The Karok Indians," *Siskiyou Pioneer and Yearbook*, vol. 4, no. 4, p. 17.

31. Lila M. O'Neale, *Yurok-Karok Basket Weavers*, University of California Publications in American Archaeology and Ethnology, vol. 32, no. 1, pp. 21-24.

32. Lottie Beck, "Karok Basketry," *Siskiyou Pioneer and Yearbook*, vol. 4, no. 4, p. 23.

33. Ibid., pp. 22-23.

34. Hazel Davis, "The Karok Indians," *Siskiyou Pioneer and Yearbook*, vol. 4, no. 4, p. 17.

35. Ibid., p. 18.

36. Ibid., p. 17.

37. C. Hart Merriam, *Ethnographic Notes on California Indian Tribes, II*, ed. and comp. by R. F. Heizer, Reports of the University of California Archaeological Survey, no. 68, p. 211.

38. John P. Harrington, *Tobacco Among the Karuk Indians of California*, p. 103.

39. Ibid.

40. Lila M. O'Neale, *Yurok-Karok Basket Weavers*, University of California Publications in American Archaeology and Ethnology, vol. 32, no. 1, p. 33.

41. Ibid., p. 35.

42. Ibid., pp. 38-41.

43. Ibid., p. 34.

44. William L. Bright, *Karok* in *Handbook of North American Indians*, R. F. Heizer, ed., vol. 8, p. 185.

45. Designs adapted from Lila M. O'Neale, *Yurok-Karok Basket Weavers*, University of California Publications in American Archaeology and Ethnology, vol. 32, no. 1, pp. 62-104 and A. L. Kroeber, *Basket Designs of the Indians of Northwestern California*, University of California Publications in American Archaeology and Ethnology, vol. 2, no. 3, pp. 116-140.

# Chapter Five

# CULTURAL ORGANIZATION

The Upriver People lived harmoniously under one of the loosest kinds of social and political organization. Curtis states that the only social division within the Karuk community was the family, while its only political division was the village.[1] There were no "chiefs." Leadership was exercised by men of wealth, on the basis of the prestige such wealth conferred upon them.[2] Wealth alone, however, did not assure a leadership position. Such individuals won the esteem of their community through assuming responsibility and demonstrating personal integrity. The wealthiest and most honorable individuals usually had good judgment, communal interest, and were dedicated to the values and laws of the group.[3]

The community as a whole was regulated and held together by the ethical values its members shared in common. Although the individual, not the group, was the primary entity, each person's ability and integrity formed a reciprocal responsibility to all other individuals. This strong belief in personal responsibility to others created an atmosphere of communal respect and stability.

## Social Bonds

Extended families included parents, unmarried daughters, sons, daughters-in-law, grandchildren, and sometimes orphan relations. Slaves and half-married men were often members of the household as well. A dwelling house served as the social center for each family.

The majority of villages had two or three dwelling houses along with a communal sweathouse and a menstrual hut. The largest villages boasted of up to fifteen family houses

*Photo 15. The Jim Pepper family. Smithsonian Institution.*

along with several communal sweathouses and menstrual huts, while the smallest Karuk villages had just one dwelling house.[4] There was no political connection between these numerous settlements, but cultural ties were strong. Many of them came together to perform the major ceremonies and dances.[5]

# Family Rituals[6]

Karuk kinsfolk participated in four major family rituals. The first honored the birth of a child. The second, called the Flower Dance, was held for adolescent girls who had experienced their first menses. The third established the tie of marriage, and the last assisted the soul of a deceased relative to pass into the afterlife.

## Birth

Since men and women were restricted from sleeping together in the dwelling house, intercourse occurred most often during the summer months when camping out to gather wild foods. Babies were usually born during the spring in the dwelling house. During pregnancy, the mother drank a tea made from vanilla grass, which they believed would make the baby smaller and easier to deliver. It was also used as a medicine for a woman who had a miscarriage.[7] During delivery, she reclined and held a strap suspended from the ceiling. She was sometimes aided by her closest female relatives. For a month after the delivery, the mother avoided cooking, traveling, and attending funerals. She also ate alone, avoided eating mammal flesh, and drank no cold water.

The Karuk weaned their children before naming them. Names were a very private matter. It was considered bad manners to use the name of a living person to his face, unless a close intimacy existed. More often nicknames were used.[8] Nowadays, the medicine man fasts for three days, then journeys to the top of a mountain to pray for a suitable name for the child. The name is often based upon a character or trait that the child displays. Boys began sleeping in the sweathouse when about ten or twelve years of age, and thus started early to learn their masculine roles.

## The Flower Dance

The Flower Dance was held on warm summer evenings for girls who had come of age during the previous year. Men and women sang and danced around the initiate, whose face was painted with bold red horizontal stripes. Kroeber says that a ring of men surrounded the maiden, a circle of women stood outside, and both groups revolved dextrally. One by one the men came to the girl from behind and danced with her. The "new" woman wore a visor of jay feathers and carried a deerhoof rattle.[9] The Karuk believed that these girls would behave the rest of their life as they did during the puberty rites. At this time, they had to gather large bundles of firewood, be industrious, and learn to obey.

Many taboos were associated with menstruating women. They were forbidden to eat or cook meat, to pound acorns, or to have sexual intercourse. The restrictions lasted from four to ten days during which they were confined to the menstrual hut. New mothers and women who had just miscarried were similarly isolated.

## Marriage

Soon after the initiation, a woman was ready for marriage. Instead of independent courtship, the affair was conducted by the father of the bride and the man who wished to buy her. Proper payment to the father of the bride was to show respect to the bride and her family. The more aristocratic the family, the larger the price paid for the bride. Although young women were appreciated for their beauty, it was more important that they possess purity, proper manners, and social graces.[10]

The Karuk allowed premarital sex, but if a woman became pregnant, she had to reveal the identity of the child's father so that he could pay an indemnity. If the man paid the fee, the child was legitimate. If the guilty party paid no fee for the woman, she and her child were ostracized by the community, for she had brought dishonor upon herself and her relatives. The Karuk considered an illegitimate child socially unacceptable, but the child was still able, by its own merit, to rise to a position of dignity and respect in the community.[11] Such children were rare.

A woman who had delivered a child out of wedlock and then led a model life by remaining closely at home and working diligently was held to be a desirable match, for she had proven her fertility. A man wanting to raise a large family might prefer to buy her instead of a virgin, who could be sterile. The price paid was not large, and generally she was sold to a rich man who already owned one or more wives.[12]

A virgin ready for marriage collected a large bride price for her family, as she was much sought after. A wealthy man might hold feasts and dances for twenty days or more after acquiring her. In most cases, a new couple went to live in the husband's parent's home, where an exchange of gifts ended the ceremony. Later the man might acquire his own house, usually nearby to the house of his parents.

The Karuk practiced levirate and sororate; that is, a widow was expected to marry her husband's brother or her sister's husband. An unfaithful or incompatible spouse of either sex could be divorced. If the woman was unfaithful, her husband could demand an indemnity from the other man or assault or kill him if he so desired. Divorces consisted of the repayment of the bride price with the compensation depending on the number of children the wife had already conceived for her husband.

A man who could only pay part of the bride price could half-marry a woman if her father granted the man permission, in which case the groom lived and worked with the father-in-law.

The Upriver People considered marriage between blood-relatives a social taboo. Descent was always paternal.

## Death

The last ritual, honoring the death of a family member, was probably the most important. The relatives of the deceased removed the body from the house through a partially dismantled wall and then purified the house with incense. For burial, the family took the corpse to a family-owned grave plot near their dwelling house, where it was washed and dentalium shells were placed in the deceased one's nose and ears. The body was then laid with the head in the upstream position and lowered into the grave with ropes. Money and other valuables were broken and buried with the deceased. Pickets lashed to a horizontal pole formed a fence around the grave. Clothes and utensils were hung on the fence and left to rot.

For five nights the male kinsman who had served as the gravedigger slept next to the grave. He and the other mourners were considered contaminated at this time. They were required to undergo a sweat and to scarify themselves, and to avoid hunting, gathering, basketmaking, travel, sex, gambling, and eating fresh meat for the duration. They also cooked fish, acorns, and other food near the grave for the five nights, so that the newly departed spirit would not go hungry and become angry.

After the five days, the ghost of the deceased was believed to journey to the sky, where an especially happy place was reserved for the wealthy and for ceremonial leaders. When a person died, it was a taboo to mention his or her name until the family formally gave the name to a newborn kin.

Many deaths occurred between 1850 and 1852, and from 1854 to 1856. In fact, there was an unusual number of deaths up until the 1900s. The declining population caused many disturbances in the Karuk lifestyle. At every major dance in the late 1800s, a Mourning Anniversary was held. This consisted of ritual weeping in remembrance of departed kinsmen.

## Community Rituals

Community rituals included the Brush Dance, held for the well-being of sick children, and the Kick Dance, held when candidates were initiated as "sucking doctors" or shamans.

### The Brush Dance[13]

The Karuk and their downstream neighbors performed the so-called Brush Dance (*iihvúna*—lit. plural dancing) for the benefit of a sickly child or infant. During the ceremony the child was held in a steam of certain herbs. Another form of the dance was designated "swinging fire," because blazing torches of pitchy spruce with salal brush tied to them were swung back and forth over the child. A tule mat covered the mother and the child to protect them from sparks while the medicine woman, or priestess, worked.

The medicine woman and the sick child's mother observed continence for the first five days of the ceremony. Early the first morning, the priestess journeyed to the woods to gather herbs and to repeat her formulas. She dressed in a maple-bark apron and deerskin skirt and wore a visor of yellowhammer tail feathers. Her hair braids were spirally wrapped with strips of fur, and her face was painted with horizontal black stripes. A virgin, who wore no special ornaments but had her face painted like the medicine woman, accompanied her.

The priestess and her assistant returned and entered the patient's house in the evening, the priestess carrying a tall staff of Douglas spruce with a leafy tip and her medicine in a small burden-basket. She planted the sapling in one corner of the fireplace and tied a bulky packet of deerskin around it. The packet supposedly contained the sickness.

Four or five girls, accompanied by the medicine woman, marched slowly around the fire, each with her hands on the shoulders of the one in front of her. They sang this verse: "going to take people along" repeatedly while gazing con-

*Photo 16. Making the medicine for the Brush Dance, Ka'tim'iin August 1989.*

*Photo 17. Medicine woman and her helper with the ailing child.*

stantly at the packet. At the end of the song, they stood in a circle facing the packet and clapped their hands, shrilly shouting "Aaaa!" while the priestess grabbed the spruce and shook it vigorously. They repeated this five times and then walked around the spruce five times while holding hands. Near the end of the last circuit, the spruce began to slowly rise up through the smokehole. As the song ended, the medicine woman grabbed it and pretended to hold it back while the girls clapped their hands and shouted as they had before. The spruce was being slowly drawn up through the roof by an unseen man on the housetop.

The priestess then transferred her medicine to a basket containing water. One of the stones heating the fire was dropped in. The mother wrapped her child in a blanket, leaving only the head exposed, and held the child's head in the rising steam. From time to time, another stone was added to the basket of water. After the steaming had progressed far enough, the priestess announced: "It is done!"

At this signal, a group of men and a few unmarried girls entered and danced to a "heavy" or slow song, bending forward at the waist, slightly flexing their knees, and striking the ground with their right heels. The dancers moved slowly to the right around the fire. Some wore broad headbands covered with woodpecker scalps, while others donned bands encircled by a row of sea lion teeth which curved outward and upward. The dancers held bunches of brush in front of their faces as they performed. The "heavy" song was followed by a "light" or quick one. After a few songs, they would retire to allow a new group of dancers to perform.

Dancers from another district or tribe then competed with the first dancers, attempting to outdo them. Now and then, the child was steamed while this continued. The medicine woman danced every so often with her staff in one hand and a tray with four upright eagle feathers, one feather to each corner, in the other. She wore several pendant strings of abalone-shell beads, which rattled rhythmically when she moved. She also sounded a crane-bone whistle. All this continued for about half the night.

The next day and night were for rest. On the third night, the steaming and dancing resumed. As the night advanced, the dancers displayed their finest regalia and discarded their branches of brush for quivers of otter filled with arrows. Near the end of the ceremony, a certain young man leaped forward and danced by himself within the circle, blowing a bone whistle. A youth and a maiden later stepped into the circle and danced facing each other, occasionally exchanging places. Each held a basket containing medicine above the child and mother.

In the late 1970s, the Karuk still held the Brush Dance on a regular basis, although it had the added function of being recreational and attracting tourists.[14]

## The Kick Dance[15]

Karuk "sucking doctors," or shamans, were practically always women. Older shamans sought girls showing other worldly qualities even before puberty, while others became shamans after a dream informed them that they must become one. In either case, the proper dream was necessary first, and it often came after much praying and crying after it. At this time, a "pain" was acquired. Pains always appeared in pairs. The first came in the initiate's first special dream or trance, while its mate would come in another dream during a later stage of the initiation.

To obtain the first pain, always the strongest, a guardian spirit had to appear. This guardian spirit, usually a dead kin, especially a woman who had been herself a shaman, but sometimes an animal such as a chicken hawk or a whale, was the source of shamanistic power. The guardian placed the pain into the dreamer, and it was upon the control of this pain that the doctor's power rested. The purpose of the Kick Dance (*piyniknik*) was to help the candidate gain control of her pain.

To become a shaman required a long and arduous course of training. The dreamers worked persistently to master their "pains," by which they could then extract from a patient the disease-bringing pains in his or her body. Necessary arrangements for the Kick Dance were made with an older shaman, usually a relative who gave instructions for free. If the shaman was not a relative, the initiate paid the instructor. Fasting, abstention from drinking, and dancing to the point of exhaustion were part of the instruction.

The first Kick Dance usually took place in the winter in the sweathouse and lasted for ten days, during which the novice fasted and danced severely under the direction of the older shaman. The newly acquired pain was thereby induced to leave the initiate's body, become exhibited, and then reswallowed by her. When the new shaman could produce the pain and return it to her body at will, success was attained.

Curtis gives an account of the dance as follows: The novice danced by standing in one place in front of the fire while flexing her knees and holding her clenched fists in front of her. She kept on dancing, ceasing only when the singers paused for a break. The purpose of the continuous dancing was to "shake up the pain" in the stomach until the novice vomited.

The candidate finally threw up the sickness and caught it in her hands, which she raised with outstretched arms. With a loud sucking in of the breath, she pretended to swallow it again. After falling into a swoon, the candidate was taken on the back of a powerful man, who held the new shaman's hands in front of his shoulders and danced. If she was heavy, another man helped to support the shaman from behind. Gradually, the shaman's senses recovered and the dance ended.

Once the new shaman finished the first Kick Dance, which had helped to "cook" her pain and make it accustomed to its new abode, she would be able to suck from others similar sicknesses. However, she must first acquire its mate.

To obtain the second pain the sucking doctor waited until the summer, when she went to a mountain summit to a

*Photo 18. Shaman Phoebe Maddox. Smithsonian Institution.*

place half enclosed with stone called the "seat." Seats were special places visited by the Ikxaréeyav long ago. There she danced and sang again, at night, until another trance occurred and the second pain was acquired. A guard, usually a family member, accompanied her to protect her from harming herself when in the trance state. After this, the shaman ran back to the river and her village where she underwent the procedures of the Kick Dance once again. This was the final stage of becoming a recognized shaman. Most shamans, in the course of their career, acquired additional pains, but these were never as potent as the first pain.

Shamans unable to capture a pain from a patient often told the sick person that they had no power over that kind of sickness, and recommended that another doctor be called for. Men of wealth sometimes sent for a distant well-known healer, such as a doctor from another tribe.

The primary duty of the sucking doctor was to cure diseases caused by "pains," which were believed to be little hostile objects that entered the body from outside, perhaps deposited there by evil spirits. Some were thought to be due to a person's "wrong-doing." In the latter case, only after the "sinner" had confessed to the doctor, within the hearing of others, would he receive help.

The shaman's technique of curing seems to have been like this. As the doctor's power came upon her, one of her pains would rise in her gorge. As she moved her mouth over the patient's body, her pain would come out of her mouth and enter the body of the patient. There it would meet with and join the patient's pain, which the doctor would then suck out, along with her own.

Another type of doctor was the herb doctor, who might be a man or a woman. The herb doctor administered herbal medicines internally or externally as needed, fumigated the patient with tobacco and plant incense, and recited magic formulas over the patient in order to induce the pain or sickness.[16] Rattlesnake bites, cuts, bruises, breaks, and fevers were usually cured in this manner. Arrowhead and bullet wounds were treated in a similar fashion, although the pain was also sucked out.

Patients paid doctors a fee before receiving treatment. If the treatment proved unsuccessful or if the patient died within the year, the doctor had to compensate the normal curing fee to the patient or the patient's survivors.[17] Sucking doctors could face the death penalty if they refused to render treatment or if they were unwilling to return payment rendered for unsuccessful treatment.

## Karuk Law[18]

The Karuk shared a standard set of laws with their downstream neighbors, the Hupa and the Yurok. This whole system was based on the concept of compensation rather than retaliation. Every offense had its own price and every invasion of privilege or property had an exact compensation. There was no offense against the community: only individuals could be wronged or blamed for wrongdoing. Sex, age, nationality, or records of previous offenses did not modify or diminish responsibility in any way.

Both the Yurok and the Karuk rated the price for killing a man of standing at fifteen strings of good dentalia, in addition to some other property, such as a daughter. The price paid for adultery or seduction was about two to three strings, and four to seven if the father accepted his illegitimate child.

The Upriver People allowed no excuse for committing a crime, but they were not unjust. Their judgment of the correct compensation was based upon moral principles which were the underlying fabric bonding the people together. After an offense was committed, only the parties involved or their representatives were entitled to settle on a compensation. After paying this fee, the offense was forgiven. If any further resentment occurred, the party who paid the fee was entitled to receive the money back.

The basic principle of Karuk law was that everything had its price, including humans. Property, both material and nonmaterial, either possessed a value set by custom or could be valued by the amount of payment made for it in previous changes of ownership. Persons possessed valuations that differed according to the amount of property they owned and other factors of social status. A slave was rated at one to two strings of dentalia, and a wife at five to ten strings by the Karuk. Dentalium shells were of different value according to their size, and payments were commonly supplemented with other treasures.

## Wealth

One of the underlying structures of Karuk society was wealth, mainly in the form of treasures or finery. The Northwestern California Indians in general placed emphasis on acquiring material goods. To obtain riches was a large task and usually only men could do so. Women could inherit wealth, but this was rare for they were a treasure themselves.

There was a variety of ways to acquire wealth. One way was to be industrious, an important thing to learn at an early age. Self-restraint and thrift were also valued. Some men never acquired wives or had few children in order to spend their time acquiring treasures. Puritanical attitudes toward sex were also favored, for sex was an enemy of wealth.[19]

Magical practices and taboos were good things to know and observe. Performing ritual songs and prayers brought success in hunting and gambling. Sorcerers were feared but not condemned.[20]

To be an affluent person meant that one owned a great deal of property in the form of money or other treasures, such as woodpecker scalps, obsidian blades, or many fishing spots. Some wealthy men owned two or more wives as well as slaves. They could host a dance when they wished and feast the participants for as long as they chose to stay.[21] During these festivals, they lent out many expensive material items so as not to appear stingy, lest poor people make bad luck for them.[22] The following is a description of wealth items.

## Money[23]

The Karuk used dentalium shell money (*ishpuk*) as a universal means of exchange, similar to the use of currency in western societies today. For most Pacific Northwest and California Indians, the dentalium shell served as the primary monetary base. Other material items were mainly valued for purposes of ornamentation.

The dentalium shells were of two species, both found buried in the sand in relatively deep water. The most abundant, *Dentalium indianorum*, was obtained through trade from the people in the British Columbia area. The rarer genus, *Dentalium hexagonum*, was obtained from the southern coast. Both shells reached the Upriver People after being carried many miles, maybe hundreds of miles, through a series of unknown nations.

The value of the shells depended on their size. They were arranged on a string in order by length and positioned with each successive shell having the butt end in the opposite direction so as not to slip inside one another. In this manner, they could be measured without being unstrung. The shell pieces on one string were usually as near as possible to one size. The general length of a string was 27½ inches long. The valuation of dentalia when not on strings was individual or by fives.

The largest dentalia were two and a half inches long and scarce. Possession of two or more of these strings, at eleven shells to a string, was enough to make a man well-known. The Karuk called the largest size of dentalium shells *pisiwawa*. The next size they called *pisiwawa afishni*, while the shortest they designated *sishareetrôopavn*. Broken shell lengths were called *apmananich*.

All other shells were regarded as insignificant next to the dentalia, which even became personified in myths. Haliotis and olivella shells were used for ornaments, but did not rate as currency. They were strung onto necklaces, worn on dresses, used as ear pendants and in the inlay of pipes, and also were common in graves.

## Woodpecker Scalps[24]

The next nearest approach to the character of money was the soft, scarlet woodpecker scalp. Two kinds of scalps were known. The larger, more valuable scalp was slightly more brilliant, called *furax* by the Karuk. The smaller woodpecker scalp was more abundant by a ratio of six to one. Woodpecker scalps were valued primarily as splendid decorative material that could be worked into magnificent headdresses or headbands as well as used for trim on other regalia.

## Deerskins[25]

Deerskins of rare coloration had the greatest value. One who possessed a pure albino deerskin with transparent hoofs was known far and wide. To part with one would have been like a king giving away his crown. Unusually light or dark deerskins were wealth items as well. Common deerskins had additional value when prepared for dance use, for the head was stuffed and woodpecker scalps were placed in the ears, eyes, throat, and tongue.

Otterskin and bearskin were also prized. The Karuk obtained otterskin from the coast and bearskin from their own territory.

## Fishing Privileges[26]

The most prolific fishing eddies were usually private property. Several individuals would rotate their use according to proportionate shares of ownership. However, single individuals sometimes owned them. Women could possess fishing rights but were not allowed to fish. No one was allowed to fish directly below a recognized fishing spot or to establish a new fishing place.

If one man used another man's eddy and was hurt there, the motto was: "He was hurt at your spot. You should pay him!" The hurt man could then receive up to one-half of the spot's privileges, even if he was not given permission to fish there in the first place.

Other locations, not privately owned, could be used by any fisherman. Each family was given a spot and a day to fish if they so desired. No one ever fished during another's time. The Karuk were never greedy with food, for it was always abundant. They divided surplus fish among families who waited at certain gathering places during the salmon run.

## Debt Slavery[27]

Slavery was an accepted institution among the Karuk but not a significant one. Only a very small percentage of the population were slaves. It occurred among the Upriver People only when a poor person sold himself to a wealthy man out of debt arising from legal difficulties, such as being unable to pay the indemnity for physical violence or the destruction of property. Slaves were never acquired through wars with neighboring tribes, because men were not taken as prisoners and women or children captured were later restored to their people when a settlement was reached. A poor man might become a slave after striking a rich man's son or after mentioning the name of a wealthy man who had died.

A slave, considered the proprietor's sole property, did such chores as making strings and nets and fishing for his master. He could have a wife, but if the couple had children, they belonged to his owner. Slaves could be redeemed and freed if their relatives repaid their debt.[28]

## Endnotes

1. Edward S. Curtis, *The North American Indian*, vol. 13, p. 60.

2. William L. Bright, *Karok* in *Handbook of North American Indians*, R. F. Heizer, ed., vol. 8, p. 184.

3. Theodora Kroeber and R. F. Heizer, *Almost Ancestors: The First Californians*, p. 52.

4. Edward S. Curtis, *The North American Indian*, vol. 13, p. 58.

5. Ibid., p. 222.

6. The section on family rituals is adapted primarily from William L. Bright, *Karok* in *Handbook of North American Indians*, R. F. Heizer, ed., vol. 8, p. 186, unless otherwise noted.

7. Sara M. Schenck and E. W. Gifford, *Karok Ethnobotany*, University of California Anthropological Records, vol. 13, no. 6, p. 380.

8. A. L. Kroeber, *Handbook of the Indians of California*, p. 107.

9. Ibid., p. 106.

10. Jack Norton, *Genocide in Northwestern California*, p. 46.

11. Ibid.

12. Edward S. Curtis, *The North American Indian*, vol. 13, p. 60.

13. Information on the Brush Dance is adapted from Edward S. Curtis, *The North American Indian*, vol. 13, pp. 44-46.

14. Gary Palmer, *Karuk World Renewal and Village Sites*.

15. Information on Shamanism is obtained from Edward S. Curtis, *The North American Indian*, vol. 13, pp. 43-44; Robert Spott and A. L. Kroeber, "Yurok Shamanism," *The California Indians: A Source Book*, R. F. Heizer and M. A. Whipple, eds., pp. 533-543; and A. L. Kroeber, *Handbook of the Indians of California*, pp. 63-68.

16. William L. Bright, *Karok* in *Handbook of North American Indians*, R. F. Heizer, ed., vol. 8, p. 188.

17. Ibid.

18. Karuk law is primarily adapted from A. L. Kroeber, "Yurok Law and Custom," *The California Indians: A Source Book*, R. F. Heizer and M. A. Whipple, eds., pp. 391-392.

19. William L. Bright, *Karok* in *Handbook of North American Indians*, R. F. Heizer, ed., vol. 8, p. 181.

20. Ibid.

21. Theodora Kroeber and R. F. Heizer, *Almost Ancestors: The First Californians*, pp. 53-54.

22. William L. Bright, *Karok* in *Handbook of North American Indians*, R. F. Heizer, ed., vol. 8, p. 181.

23. Primarily adapted from A. L. Kroeber, "Yurok Law and Custom," *The California Indians: A Source Book, R. F. Heizer and M. A. Whipple, eds., pp. 394-396.*

24. Ibid., p. 397.

25. Ibid., pp. 397-398.

26. Ibid., pp. 405-406.

27. Ibid.

28. Harold E. Driver, *Culture Element Distributions: Northwest California*, University of California Anthropological Records, vol. 1, no. 6, p. 357.

# Chapter 6

# CEREMONIES

Kroeber proposes that the Karuk and their downstream neighbors held annual sacred ceremonies in a closed system of Native American religion, comparable to the secret Hamatsa initiations and performances of the northern Pacific Coast tribes and the Kuksu cult of central California. This system, although greatly variable in detail, had a single coherent scheme. It aimed at the reestablishment or refixing of the world, the observance of first fruits, in order to prevent in the coming year the occurrence of disasters, such as the failure of the salmon run or the acorn crop, floods, disease, and famine.[1]

When the world was first created, the Karuk say that the Ikxaréeyav acted in certain ways and accomplished certain results before departing or transforming themselves. These same ways were ordained by the Ikxaréeyav to be followed by the Karuk. Medicine men, designated as "spirit people" (*ikxaréeyav arra*), who were commonly descendants of prestigious households, represented the immortals and preserved their preordained ways.[2] Thus was the order of the world maintained. Because human welfare was at stake, the medicine men performed the ceremonies with great solemnity and attention to detail so that the Ikxaréeyav would not be offended.

The Karuk were deeply religious, and their religion was at the core of their way of life. Norton says that the Indians of northwestern California began and ended their days with songs that were generally prayers. They were constantly urged by both the internal and external elements of their way of life to "keep a good heart," to "not think badly of people," to "be kind and respectful of the old."[3]

When two young white ladies from the Bureau of Indian Affairs observed the Karuk in 1908, they wrote of them: "an Indian characteristic that impressed us very much was what we would call good breeding, a code of manners and feeling that stood out in sharp contrast to the lower social level of the average pioneer white man."[4]

Traditional ceremonies and dances held by the Karuk and their downstream neighbors in the late 1800s included the World Renewal Ceremony, the First Salmon Ceremony, the Deerskin Dance, and the Jump Dance, as well as lesser events such as the War Dance. The Deerskin Dance and the War Dance were always held in conjunction with the World Renewal Ceremony. The Karuk say that there was no connection between the Jump Dance and the First Salmon Ceremony which were both held at Ameekyáaraam. Participation in the ceremonies was limited to certain individuals, while the dances could be observed and attended by all.[5] The concept of renewal or reestablishing the world for another year was important to all of the major ceremonies and dances, except the Jump Dance.

Only certain villages could properly hold these rituals because of their essential connection with the immediate local environment.[6] They were usually the largest villages and had an important name or history associated with the deeds of the Ikxaréeyav. These ceremonial villages were inseparable from intangible cultural values and could thus link all the surrounding villages into a competitive display of regalia, cooperative dancing, feasting, and ceremonial participation.

The Upriver People wanted their world to be ordered, stable, and permanent. Everything had its proper place in the order of things. A good life was one that was balanced between the spiritual and the mundane. It was believed that the renewal rites would help to make this so.[7]

Among the ninety Karuk villages recalled by a Karuk informant in 1860,[8] only four held annual renewal ceremonies. The World Renewal Ceremony and the associated Deerskin Dance were held at Inaam, Panámniik, and Ka'tim'iin. Both Inaam and Ka'tim'iin were sites of the War Dance, and the Karuk performed the First Salmon Ceremony and the Jump Dance only at Ameekyáaraam.[9]

When ceremonies and dances occurred, the people used the larger towns and neighboring villages for gatherings and feasts. The dances were performed repetitively, as well as competitively in regard to display, by several groups of dancers, each representing a nearby settlement.[10] Expensive regalia for these performances were provided by wealthy individuals.

Sacred houses, hybrids between the dwelling house and the sweathouse, were found only in ceremonial villages and were used ceremonially during these religious events.[11] At other times of the year, they were occupied by a family, except for the sacred house at Ka'tim'iin, which was reserved exclusively for ceremonial usage. Inaam had no sacred house and no other house was used during its World Renewal Ceremony.

During the ceremonies, men used certain sweathouses for purification purposes. If dancing indoors, the dances occurred at one particular living house, while another house would be used by the dancers to array themselves or to practice.[12]

Both men and women wore elaborate clothing during these festivities. Women wore fancy shell necklaces and dresses decorated with strings of digger pine nuts, abalone, olivella shells, bear-lily braids, and other small treasures. Women functioning as assistants to the medicine men donned maple-bark skirts. Both sexes painted their faces with red or white minerals mixed with grease. Men wore headdresses and bandoleers decorated with woodpecker scalps and other feathers. Their pierced ears and noses sometimes carried ornaments.[13]

# The World Renewal Ceremony[14]

The Karuk dedicated their most important religious practice, the World Renewal Ceremony, called *irahiv* or *pikyavish* by the Karuk, to the Ikxaréeyav in order to have an abundance of food and good health and fortune in the coming year. The people of Inaam held the Pikyavish in August, while those at Ka'tim'iin and Panámniik held it in September. The Karuk always began the ceremony ten days before the disappearance of the waning moon. The Ka'tim'iin and Panámniik ceremonies were nearly synchronized, although the climax of the Ka'tim'iin ceremony followed the climax of the Panámniik ceremony by one to three days.

There were three parts to this religious performance. First, for ten days, the medicine man, or priest, who could be any man belonging to the village where the ceremony was held who knew the rituals, prayed and fasted and performed special rituals. Then, on the last night of the waning moon, he kept an all night vigil by the sacred sand pit (*yuhpit*). The vigil was accompanied and followed by the Deerskin Dance or its imitation. At Inaam and Ka'tim'iin the War Dance was part of the dance ritual. The third part of the ceremony consisted of the anticlimactic retreat of the medicine man and other dance officials for five to ten days. In all the rituals, the priest represented the Ikxaréeyav, who had once performed the same rites in the same places.

During the first, or private part of the ceremony, the medicine man fasted, abstained from sleep, and remained much of the time in the sacred sweathouse. He blew tobacco crumbs to the spirits of old, smoked tobacco, and burned angelica root incense. He also made visits to sacred spots in a specified order, where he recited segments of a long, traditional formula. Young men accompanied the medicine man at this time and competed in archery contests (*ishriv*) not far away while the priest performed his duties. Curtis says that the archers shouted continuously in order to encourage the medicine man who was weak from fasting.[15] Should the medicine man become exhausted, he could ask another to replace him as priest for the duration of the ceremony.

One of Drucker's informants said that at Panámniik singing took place each night of the ceremony except for the last
two or three nights, when the Deerskin Dance or a feast was
held. During the singing, all of the men, including the
medicine man, had to sit down and draw their knees up so
their elbows rested upon them. They could extend only one
leg at a time. Occasionally, a man might stand for a few
minutes to rest. The singing came to a halt in the middle of
the night to allow the medicine man a few hours of sleep
before resuming his morning rituals.

The medicine man arose to pray, or to recite a formula,
before dawn. He then bathed in the river. This occupied most
of the morning. When he finished these tasks, the medicine
man entered the sacred hut and greased his body with deer
tallow (one of Gifford's informants said that deer marrow, not
deer tallow, was used) so the bushes would not scratch him.
He painted the lower part of his face red, with black marks
on his cheeks, and drew black bands above and below his
elbows and knees. After slipping on a pair of moccasins, he
placed his pipe, tobacco, and fire drill into a large Jump
Dance basket (víkapuh) and, with basket in hand, set out for
the first sacred spot.

Each day the medicine man visited one special spot in the
nearby hills and recited given formulas. Everything he did
as he visited these sites was prescribed, even his mode of
walking. He had to go uphill and downhill and through the
brush by as direct a route as possible. He could not swing
his arms freely but had to hold them close to his sides. He
stepped with care, for he could neither drag his feet nor
stumble.

When the medicine man arrived at the sacred spot, a
small circular clearing in the brush, he first cleared away the
year's accumulation of leaves and twigs. After he had gathered a pile of wood, he ignited some tinder on a small flat
stone with his fire drill, and then placed the stone with its
kindled tinder under the wood. While the fire burned, the
medicine man sat and smoked his pipe. He did not pray at
this time. After the fire had died down, usually near to dusk,

he removed the small stone from the ashes and threw it on a pile of other stones that had been used in a similar manner in previous years.

Returning to the sacred house, the medicine man put away his paraphernalia and went to bathe in the river. In the sacred house, once again, he partook of his first and only meal of the day, consisting of dried salmon and acorn mush, served to him by a special woman cook, called *ikyávaan*. Then he went to the sweathouse for the night's singing.[16]

The procedure of the following days was much the same, except that new spots were visited and some new acts were performed. Variations took place in the secondary elements of the World Renewal Ceremony depending upon the place it was held and the medicine man who volunteered to perform the rituals. Ka'tim'iin, for example, placed more emphasis on the archery contests than Panámniik. At Inaam there was no sacred house; instead, the construction of a half-circle of stones at the mouth of Clear Creek a month prior to the ceremony was significant.

Certain renewal-type acts were performed by the medicine man during the ceremony. It is probable that, like the Yurok, he partially rebuilt or repaired the sacred house, symbolizing the restrengthening of the world. On the climactic, or tenth, night of the ceremony, the medicine man built a fire by the sacred sand pit, which was rebuilt by a former priest (*ipnipavan*). The world was straightened by kindling the new fire at the yuhpit. When the medicine man left the sacred house to go to the yuhpit, the ipnipavan preceded him, shouting "Kaiko aksanwa!", which warned the people to hide or cover their faces. To look at the medicine man or the fire at this time was a taboo (*aksanwa*). The medicine man kept an all-night vigil at the sand pit on this last night of the waning moon. He stood all of the time while offering prayers to the Ikxaréeyav. The people feasted and danced while the priest stood.

*Photo 19. The White Deerskin Dance at Orleans around the turn of the century. Humboldt State University Library.*

## The Deerskin Dance[17]

The purpose of the Deerskin Dance, *vuhvuha*, according to one of Gifford's informants, was to help keep the priest awake as he stood by the yuhpit on the last night of the Pikyavish. It also created a chance for wealthy people to publicly display their treasures, which were used to lavishly decorate the dancers. At the time of the dance, the "dance owner," always a wealthy man, offered a gift of dentalia on behalf of the deceased souls of the preceding year to friends who were generous contributors of dance regalia. Older spectators wept when they saw regalia displayed that had once belonged to departed relatives.

The Karuk held the Deerskin Dance only at the end of the World Renewal Ceremony, when the acorn harvest time and the salmon season coincided. It was not held annually. Every year that the real Deerskin Dance was not performed the imitation Deerskin Dance (*vuhvuhi istava*) was substituted in its place. Mary Ike, an informant for Kroeber and Gifford in 1942, claimed to have seen the real Deerskin Dance only five times during her ninety years.

Fancy regalia worn during the Deerskin Dance included albino deerskins as well as wolf and otter skins. The Karuk used eagle tail feathers as hair ornaments and set beaver teeth and sea lion teeth in their headbands. They also carried beautiful flint and obsidian blades. To protect the obsidian from damage on the journey to the dance place they were carried in basket cradles. When performing the imitation dance, the dancers carried foliage in place of deerskins, and sticks and stones instead of obsidian. Wealthy people were encouraged to attend the dances, even though distant from their homes, for they were honored contributors.

In 1860, Curtis's informant participated in the Deerskin Dance at Ka'tim'iin. He reported that the dancers spent the first evening dancing on the sandbar, one set of dances performed by each dance group. The next morning, they repeated the performance. After an early supper, the dancers moved to a level surface on the hill where they danced late into the night, and continued the next day until nearly sunset. At the end of the dance, a feast was served, after which everyone returned to their homes.[18]

Two to thirty or more separate dances were enacted each day. The performers, all men, stood abreast of each other, carefully ranked in a prescribed place. They stepped slowly to plaintive, wordless tunes sung by one to three dancers in the middle of the line.

To lessen the monotony, the number of dancers would be slowly but steadily increased, as well as the energy of the performances and the elaborateness of the apparel. The dancers worked to create a heightened effect. The Karuk also introduced minor variations to the dance, such as changes in locale by means of progressive stations in a journey, dancing in boats, or including special figures and effects in the grand finale.

*Photo 20. The White Deerskin Dance at Ka'tim'iin. Humboldt State University Library.*

Many villages did not take part in the Deerskin Dance. Sometimes the reason for not participating was poverty. However, this was not usually the determining factor since most villages had individuals who possessed wealth and even valuable deerskins and other regalia. These valuables were rented to individuals in other villages who did wish to participate.[19]

# The War Dance[20]

The origin of the War Dance (*thivtap*) is attributed to Ikxaréeyav coyote who lived at Orleans. It occurred ritually in imitation of a real war dance as part of the World Renewal Ceremony at Ka'tim'iin and Inaam. The people of Panámniik, as well as the Yurok and the Hupa, never performed it, except as a real war dance of victory or at a settlement of indemnity for the slain. At Inaam, the Karuk performed the imitation War Dance annually before the medicine man began his sacred duties, and he could participate in it if he wished. The Karuk at Ka'tim'iin performed it only after the Deerskin Dance, the day after the priest terminated his duties, as the terminal dance of the Pikyavish.

The dancers began their performance in the late afternoon, as the sun descended behind the mountains. Dancers sometimes entered the dance flat from the woods shouting and firing guns, or they might carry only branches. In the days before firearms, they carried bows and arrows. The dancers sometimes tinted their faces red with moistened alder bark. The men danced side by side, as in the Deerskin Dance, but all sang.

Gifford believes the imitation War Dance to be a recent addition to the World Renewal Ceremony at Inaam and Ka'tim'iin. The reason for the addition is not known. Wars were not common among the Northwestern California Indians until the miners moved in and created havoc. What were referred to as "wars" among the Karuk and their neighbors were actually feuds caused by a killing, physical injury, or damage to property. Such feuds could be settled with the aid of a go-between, who was paid for his services.[21]

After a compensation was arranged, the opposing parties would face each other. The men on each side then performed an armed "war dance" in front of the settlement money while singing valiant songs to insult the other side. A medicine man would recite the proper formula over the money, and it would exchange hands as agreed. The settlement concluded with this exchange and the breaking of weapons.[22]

There were risks that new fighting might break out, but this usually did not occur because each man knew he must control his emotions after the proper payment had been made.[23] Women often successfully restrained men from further violence.

When the eventuality of battle arose, warriors usually donned armor and carried bows and arrows and short spears. Bows for war and hunting were made of yew wood. The Karuk glued deer sinew to the back of the bow's green wood and bound it with a cord wrapping, creating a permanent reverse curve which added greatly to its pull. For battle the arrows were tipped with barbed heads of flint or obsidian. The Karuk used short spears with large obsidian blades for short range thrusting. Besides this, each man wore one white eagle feather in his hair. In modern times, men stuck the feather into a white man's hat.

In the 1800s a war broke out between the Karuk and the Tolowa when Wakhtek, a Yurok village, was holding the Deerskin Dance.[24] Visitors were attending the dance from the middle Klamath River, or Karuk country, and from the Smith River, or Tolowa country. A Tolowa woman became enamored with a Karuk youth and followed him to his village. Later, one of the woman's kin came to the Karuk and demanded an indemnity claiming the youth had damaged her family reputation, because she had been taken without payment. The Karuk refused to pay, for the woman had followed the boy herself and had gone of her own will. The Karuk finally decided to pay the Tolowa man and he started home. On his way home, however, he was waylaid and killed.

In response, a war-party of the Tolowa crossed the mountains and attacked the village of Ameekyáaraam. Most of the people of Ameekyáaraam were in the nearby hills as part of the celebration of the First Salmon Ceremony. Even though the raiders found only a few old people and the medicine man at the village, they attacked them. But one of the old people ran to the other villagers with the news. At once the men swarmed down and drove the Tolowa warriors off. The Karuk claimed that only one Tolowa reached home. The others fell victim to various disasters, such as grizzly bear attacks, rattlesnake bites, and falling trees! The Karuk and Tolowa finally made up after indemnities were paid to the families of those killed in the affair.

## The First Salmon Ceremony[25]

The Karuk held the annual First Salmon Ceremony only at Ameekyáaraam during Ikrivkihan (The Sixth Moon), which occurred in late March or early April, commencing it ten days before the dark of the moon. It lasted for ten days, followed by ten days of retreat. This ceremony, also called *iduramva*, meaning "people run away and hide," seems to have been the Karuk's only harvest festival. It meant that the season for fishing had come; the people could once again collect salmon and steelhead, their main sustenance.

Eating fresh fish prior to this ceremony was strictly forbidden. Any person who did not practice self-restraint and ate salmon or steelhead before the ceremony risked being drowned on the following day or being killed by a rock rolling down the mountainside. A person was not supposed to even touch a steelhead before the ceremony. These taboos had to be followed or "the world would fall apart."

An interesting element of this ceremony was the "crooked immortals" (*ikxaréeyakuna*), ten sacred stones set on top of the Ameekyáaraam sacred sweathouse, Ikriripan, so as to "look" downriver during the ceremony. The stones were one foot long, red, and bent in an obtuse angle. During the ceremony the medicine man blew unburned tobacco from his hand as an offering to the stones. There were only two of these stones left in 1942, and one of Gifford's informants said that when all of these stones disappear, the Karuk will cease to exist.

On the first morning of the ceremony, certain people watched the sun from the sacred dwelling house (*veenáram*). After the sun rose above a certain clump of trees on the ridge behind Asánaamkarak, they made a fire to warm Ikriripan's stone slab floor. The medicine man then swept the floor, while someone else swept the trail he was to walk on to the creek so he could take a bath. As he swept, the medicine man said: "I'm sweeping all the disease away. I'm sweeping it away from one end of the earth to the other."

During the first nine days, or the private part of the ceremony, the medicine man did this ritual sweeping and bathing every morning and in the evening when the fire died down. Someone always swept the trail to his bathing place. When bathing, the medicine man exclaimed, "I am getting into salmon blood!" He would then go to the sacred dwelling house to eat, and afterward would again go to bathe. While he ate, the medicine man could not hear any noise, or else he would stop eating. He spent most of the day in the sweathouse praying for an abundance of salmon, acorns, and other food in the coming year. Every night men joined him in the sweathouse to sing about the salmon and steelhead.

On the first day only, the medicine man walked uphill with an elk-horn chisel and stone maul to cut a madrone pole. He then carried the young tree back down on his left shoulder to a pepperwood tree near the sweathouse and left it there to rot.

On the ninth day, an assistant medicine man and a young virgin, the wood-gatherer, entered the ceremony. The virgin crossed the river on a ferry from Asánaamkarak to Ameekyáaraam.

At about four the next morning, on the day commencing the dark of the waning moon, a group of men would shout "Iduramva!" (Go and hide!) ten times, first at the sweathouse and then at other places. At this time, people left for the day so they would not see the sacred fire or its smoke.

Two men then ferried the virgin back to Asánaamkarak where she chopped up a dead madrone for firewood and carried it and its chips back to the sacred fire site at the river's edge. One of the men ferried her again to Ameekyáaraam. There, she entered the sacred dwelling house and busied herself so she would not peek at the fire.

The medicine man and his assistant now crossed the river to Asánaamkarak. The assistant paddled while the medicine man sat quietly. Before embarking he puffed his pipe twice on the Ameekyáaraam side, blowing smoke to all directions while praying. On the Asánaamkarak side, he repeated the smoking ritual once.

After arriving at the fire site, the assistant leveled a place for the fire. The medicine man used a willow-root drill and cedar-bark tinder to start a flame. The assistant tended it with the madrone wood that the virgin had cut. Both avoided looking at the ascending smoke. They then proceeded to cook the first salmon. When the salmon was half-baked, the assistant ate it until he vomited, for the half-cooked flesh made him sick. This brought him good luck. The two men then built an altar with rocks, and, after bathing, returned to Ikriripan, staying in the structure for ten more days.

Upon their return to Ameekyáaraam, men sang songs, while someone went to the edge of the nearby bluff and shouted to the people, "Come home!" The virgin went to bathe in the creek. Any woman could enter the sweathouse at this time to stay with and cook for the medicine men for the next ten days. This brought her luck, but she must remain continent. The people returned from the hills by evening.

Five days after the ceremony of eating the first salmon, the virgin wood-gatherer emerged from the sacred living house where she had been in retreat. She gathered two river cobbles, heated them, and boiled salmon with them. The water was tossed into the river along with the small stones in the cooking basket that had been used to cook acorn soup for the priests. After this was done, the people could prepare salmon in the usual manner.

For two to three months after the ceremony, as after the World Renewal Ceremony, the officiating medicine man could not touch boards, because they were used to bury the dead. He also had to eat seated and could not drink water.

The Kepel weir, located downriver in Yurok country, was a well-known location for catching salmon at the peak of their spawning season. The site was said by the Karuk to be where the Yurok habitually build a weir. Kroeber called it the "greatest mechanical undertaking of the tribes in question." Redwood trees grew at this weir, which was twenty-five miles downriver from Karuk country and about seven miles above the Pacific. Many expressive acts of magic with associated playful enactments were performed at the Kepel weir site. Although the Karuk came only as visitors, many of these rituals seem to have derived from them.

## The Jump Dance[26]

The Jump Dance, held biennially, took place in July at Ameekyáaraam several months after the First Salmon Ceremony and had nothing to do with the latter. The Jump Dance was held, one informant said, in order to prevent sickness, bring happiness, and make good weather. A Yurok elder may have given the deeper meaning of all such dances: "When man and the world become unbalanced, then we must dance the great dances, rhythmically stamping upon the earth, exchanging with it and balancing all that brings health, strength, food, honor, good luck, and happiness for all."[27]

In preparation for the Jump Dance, the rich man who gave it inquired as to who would be the priest or medicine man, called ixmeehváthaan, for this event. He would have to stay in the Ikriripan sweathouse for the first nine days of the ceremony, and he could not ask to be replaced if he tired as could the officiating priest of the World Renewal Ceremony.

*Photo 21. Emily Ike and Jasper Donahue in traditional costume, the latter wearing a ceremonial headdress made of woodpecker scalps used in the Jump Dance. Siskiyou County Museum.*

Any man who wished to officiate as the medicine man could do so. He received no payment, but if he could stand the ordeal of fasting and sweating and observed all the taboos, he would have good fortune afterward.

The ixmeehváthaan began his ten day fast on the first day of the Jump Dance. During this time, he stayed alone in the sacred sweathouse, smoking tobacco, and reciting certain prayers and formulas in order to bring luck or money to himself, to provide an abundance of food for his people, and to help overcome sickness in the world. When sleeping at night, he rested his head on a wooden pillow. His only visitor was the young virgin who cooked his meal, which he took every other day, usually just before sunset, while he sat on a little platform under a pepperwood tree. However, some medicine men abstained from food even longer. One informant who had served as the Jump Dance priest in 1895 said that he had taken food only after the fifth day. The longer the medicine man fasted, the more luck he would have.

Each morning for ten days the medicine man collected wood to build a fire in the sacred sweathouse. Sometimes, while doing this, he would wail in remembrance of departed relatives. After building the fire, he swept the stone platform outside the hut. As he swept, he exclaimed, "I am sweeping away sickness!" While bathing at a pool in the creek (well away from the river), he said, "I wish that I shall have good luck!" As he swam in the pool, he said, "I am swimming in the upstream ocean!" The upstream ocean, Kayuras, was the mythical source of dentalium shells.

At dusk on the first evening and at dawn the following morning only, the medicine man fished for dentalia from the rock called Asatak opposite the mouth of the Salmon River. He fished for only a few minutes, using a fishing pole from which he dangled one shell on a line into the water. He left the fishing pole at this rock. No one could watch the medicine man fish, lest they ruin his luck.

For the first nine days of the Jump Dance, the dancers performed daily at Ameekyáaraam. There might be as many as four groups of dancers in the Jump Dance, each performing for a dance owner, who kept a camp where he offered hospitality. Owners competed to display the best dance. Any man wishing to dance could do so.

The leader of the dance group, decked out in fancy regalia, faced the line of dancers, all of whom were men, except for two virgins who danced at each end of the line. All the men held flexible, twined basketry wallets (vikapuh) with warps of sedge in their right hands. They swung these up in the air and brought them down synchronously to their sides as they jumped. After repeating this three or four times, the men sat down on stones behind them. Next, the dancers set their basketry wallets on the ground in front of them and all jumped up together, holding hands.

After the fifth day, the men exchanged their basketry wallets for eight-foot fir poles painted with red and black bands. These they leaned forward and back in unison with each jump. Girls, wearing their finest regalia, danced in the center of the line and did not hold poles. When the dancing was over, the men jabbed their poles into the ground and broke off the tips to use as medicine while hunting, "to prevent grizzly bear attacks," they said.

In the afternoon of the ninth day, the medicine man came out of the sweathouse and went to the Ameekyáaraam dance grounds. The dancers separated into two lines and he passed between them on his way to the bathing area. Upon his return, he again passed through the dancers. Donning a small headband made of woodpecker feathers, he sat down behind the dancers for a while. Then he went in turns to sweep the dance places that the dancers would use that night. The medicine man swept at each place until the dancers arrived, and two performances were held at each place. This continued until the dancers and the medicine man arrived at Asatak.

On the tenth day, the dancers displayed their most elaborate regalia. They competed at Asatak until mid-afternoon. At this time, the medicine man removed the fishing pole from its hiding place behind the rock. Certain girls brought him a meal, which signified the end of the ixmeehváthaan's duties.

## Decline of the Ceremonies[28]

The social disorganization experienced by the Karuk due to the incoming miners and settlers made the ceremonies difficult to maintain. Anglos threatened the ceremonies and burned many of the villages. Medicine men began to complain that the world had been "made wrong," and they took offense when Anglicized Karuk ridiculed them. Ceremonies became shorter and more abbreviated, and some came to a halt when there were no more medicine men who would recite the prayers or conduct the rituals.

As traditional values weakened, the Karuk sought for anything that would reaffirm their vanishing lifestyle. This led to their acceptance of the Ghost Dance in 1871 from the

Shasta. This dance became popular with many California Indians. Those participating believed that the world would soon end and all of their dead kin would be resurrected with them into a new world where traditional values were restored. The Ghost Dance was held at Inaam, Ka'tim'iin, and Ameekyáaraam in 1871, but it made no lasting impression.

By 1943, ceremonies had ceased at almost all of the Karuk's chief ceremonial sites. The last Jump Dance was held in 1895 or 1899. In 1907, violence occurred during the Deerskin Dance at Orleans. In 1908, the last officiating medicine man at Ka'tim'iin claimed that the world had been "made wrong."[29] Four years later, in 1912, the last medicine man at Panámniik ceased holding the Deerskin Dance because the Anglicized Karuk made fun of it. It was held for the last time in Ka'tim'iin that year. The First Salmon Ceremony probably was also abandoned in 1912. World Renewal ceremonies continued at Ka'tim'iin and Inaam until 1943, and were then abandoned until their revival at Inaam in the 1950s and at Ka'tim'iin in 1970.

## Endnotes

1. A. L. Kroeber and E. W. Gifford, *World Renewal: A Cult System of Native Northwest California*, University of California Anthropological Records, vol. 13, no. 1, p. 1.

2. Ibid., p. 6.

3. Jack Norton, *Genocide in Northwestern California*, p. 27.

4. Mary E. Arnold and Mabel Reed, *In the Land of the Grasshopper Song*, foreword.

5. A. L. Kroeber and E. W. Gifford, *World Renewal: A Cult System of Native Northwest California*, University of California Anthropological Records, vol. 13, no. 1, p. 3.

6. Ibid.

7. Ibid., p. 5.

8. Edward S. Curtis, *The North American Indian*, vol. 13, pp. 222-225.

9. A. L. Kroeber and E. W. Gifford, *World Renewal: A Cult System of Native Northwest California*, University of California Anthropological Records, vol. 13, no. 1, pp. 6-7.

10. Ibid., p. 3.

11. Ibid., pp. 3, 6.

12. Ibid.

13. William L. Bright, *Karok* in *Handbook of North American Indians*, R. F. Heizer, ed., vol. 8, p. 184.

14. Adapted from A. L. Kroeber and E. W. Gifford, *World Renewal: A Cult System of Native Northwest California*, University of California Anthropological Records, vol. 13, no. 1, unless otherwise noted.

15. Edward S. Curtis, *The North American Indian*, vol. 13, p. 62.

16. Philip Drucker, *A Karuk World-Renewal Ceremony at Panaminik*, University of California Publications in American Archaeology and Ethnology, vol. 35, no. 3, pp. 23-25.

17. Most information obtained from A. L. Kroeber and E. W. Gifford, *World Renewal: A Cult System of Native Northwest California*, University of California Anthropological Records, vol. 13, no. 1, pp. 31-33.

18. Edward S. Curtis, *The North American Indian*, vol. 13, p. 62.

19. Ibid., p. 61.

20. Information obtained from A. L. Kroeber and E. W. Gifford, *World Renewal: A Cult System of Native Northwest California*, University of California Anthropological Records, vol. 13, no. 1, p. 33, unless otherwise noted.

21. William L. Bright, *Karok* in *Handbook of North American Indians*, R. F. Heizer, ed., vol. 8, p. 185.

22. Ibid.

23. Theodora Kroeber and R. F. Heizer, *Almost Ancestors: The First Californians*, p. 53.

24. Adapted from Edward S. Curtis, *The North American Indian*, vol. 13, p. 59.

25. Adapted primarily from A. L. Kroeber and E. W. Gifford, *World Renewal: A Cult System of Native Northwest California*, University of California Anthropological Records, vol. 13, no. 1, pp. 35-40.

26. Ibid., pp. 40-47.

27. Cited in Jack Norton, *Genocide in Northwestern California*, p. 13.

28. Gary Palmer, *Karok World Renewal and Village Sites*, pp. 15-17, used extensively in this section.

29. Mary E. Arnold and Mabel Reed, *In the Land of the Grasshopper Song*, p. 122.

## Chapter 7

# HISTORY

The earliest record of any white men to pass through present-day Siskiyou County was in 1827. That winter a party of trappers from the Hudson Bay Company, under Alexander Roderick McLeod, came down the Oregon coast, moved inland, crossed the Klamath River just north of Yreka, and passed down the Shasta Valley on their way to the Sacramento Valley. This route soon became well-traveled by trappers, journeying from Vancouver to California and back, and other immigrants.[1] It is possible that the Karuk may have met some of the wide-ranging Hudson Bay Company traders in the early part of the nineteenth century, but if so the contact had little effect. Indian Ned, who was born near Clear Creek around 1823, said that he could remember the first encounter with white men about 1843, when his people befriended a group of shipwrecked travelers who were making their way to Oregon.[2]

A party of trappers with Thomas McKay entered the Scott Valley in 1836. He was said to be generous and just to the native inhabitants, who, in turn, treated him and his men with great hospitality. In one month they trapped 1,800 beavers along both forks of the Scott River.[3]

After the discovery of gold in California in 1848, immigrants and miners of all kinds began to pour into California. In the summer of 1849, Major Pearson B. Reading and his men crossed the Coast Range to the Trinity River, where they found a bar rich in gold. Each of his men claimed to be easily making forty dollars a day. A report of his trip appeared in the *Placer Times* of Sacramento later that year. By fall more groups of miners arrived to work the banks of the Trinity. In the following year thousands of newcomers entered the region in search of gold, exploring up the Klamath and Trinity rivers from the coast as well as entering the Klamath, Salmon, and Scott rivers from the east. By June 1850, a party of miners reached 'Athithúfvuunupma (Happy Camp) for the first time, where they claimed that the Indians became so hostile they had to turn back.[4] One year later a mining camp was established there, in July 1851.[5]

The miners did not come onto the middle course of the Klamath River until 1850 because of its remote location. In that year, however, three hundred miners claimed land upon the Klamath and Salmon rivers.[6] Hundreds more soon followed.

The Karuk greatly outnumbered the newcomers at first and were gracious and kind to them. They were helpful as guides, in crossing streams, and in a myriad of other ways, for the Karuk respected these people as they did all others.

These feelings of friendliness soon faded when the miners gave the mighty and unfortunate cry: "There's gold in these here hills!" The news of the California gold rush had spread quickly across the nation and beyond. Large droves of miners began to flow into the state from all over the world. The worst, the most unscrupulous, of American immigrant society was let loose upon northern California. In 1852, 2,240 people migrated into Siskiyou County. In April 1852, Redick McKee wrote to the governor of California to inform him of the Indian-miner conflict. In one incident, he relates that thirty or forty Karuk were murdered "almost in cold blood" by miners from Happy Camp.[7]

By the end of 1851, according to the population estimates of S. F. Cook, over half of the Karuk tribe had died off.[8] The Karuk community had been devastated by disease, especially syphilis. The rivers had been contaminated with muddy water washed in from the mines, and the Karuk, no longer able to catch the same amount of fish as in previous years, were starving. The miners, wanting the land only for what it could produce—gold—were not about to let any Indians interfere with their fortunes. They shot Karuk men and raped their women. Some were sold into slavery, which

*Photo 22. Sandy Bar Bob and Grace Nicholson (of Pasadena) in a canoe. Humboldt State University Library.*

was a common fate for many of the Indians in California at this time.

Once friendly in feeling and demeanor, the Upriver People soon began to show signs of discontent and dislike. They grew suspicious and considered the miners unwelcome intruders. The Karuk found that the newcomers had little morality or consideration for others. Young girls blushed with shame and shrank back in horror when miners stared lustfully at them. Without wishing to understand Northwestern California Culture, the miners and other immigrants decided that the Karuk were "just a bunch of savages"—little higher than animals.

At times, the newcomers (mostly miners) were outright ruthless, and plans were made to intimidate and exterminate the Indians. Hostilities and fighting followed. The Karuk suffered tragic losses during such outbreaks of violence. In the summer of 1852, a group of miners and other unfriendly newcomers blamed the Indians for some cattle that were found dead. The Karuk explained that the cattle had eaten poisonous weeds. An attempt was made to deprive them of guns that had been sold to them at very high prices. The result was fighting in which losses were sustained on both sides. In retaliation the white men burned Karuk villages from Orleans to a point above the mouth of the Salmon River. The Karuk were forced to flee to the hills. The white men then constructed cabins and farms where Karuk village sites had been. Panámniik, an important ceremonial center, was made into a miners' camp at this time, and the town of Orleans was founded there.[9]

The years between 1850 and 1854 were a period of constant transition in northwestern California. Mining towns, as well as farming and manufacturing communities, sprang up in distant and remote places throughout the region. Although the Indian population, in many places, still exceeded that of the immigrants, the newcomers increased rapidly. No sooner did the Indians move than Americans told them: "Move on!"

To the disadvantage of the Indians, the white people did not understand Native American culture. The Indian religion and way of life were outlandish to the newcomers. Goddard wrote in 1901, "It is largely this undercurrent of deep religious feeling that makes the life and deeds of the Indian seem so strange to the white man."[10]

The Americans, whether intentionally or not, propagated genocide among the Karuk. They raped their women, infected them with unknown diseases, destroyed the habitats where fish and game had once been plentiful, and outright murdered hundreds of individuals. The Karuk tried to defend themselves, but they had neither the power nor the means to drive all of these newcomers away.

During the winter of 1852 through 1853, the citizens of Orleans had many conflicts with the Karuk. On December 9, 1852, some Anglos (mostly miners) set out to destroy a number of Karuk villages. The Karuk defended themselves and three miners were shot to death. This frightened the miners, who then began to spread the rumor that the Indians could muster over 3,000 warriors armed with rifles and six-shooters. The citizens of Orleans pleaded for government troops to come and protect them. The motto at Orleans became: "Burn all rancherias where guns have been found." On January 27, the *Humboldt Times* reported that the citizens of Orleans, after holding a meeting to discuss the "Indian problem," voted to kill on sight any Indian possessing a gun.[11]

On January 17, 1854, a notice was sent to A. M. Rosborough, Special Indian Agent to northern California, stating that miners were going about shooting down Indians wherever they could find them, attacking them at their fishing spots and in their homes. These miners not only murdered young men but also children, women, and old people. During another incident, in which the miners in Tolowa country were bent on another shooting spree, a portion of the settlers, disgusted by the lawlessness of the marauders, stopped them from carrying out their intention.[12]

That same year, the Indians of Siskiyou County fell victim to a lack of wild game and fish, because the newcomers had hunted the animals to near extinction and destroyed the spawning sites of the steelhead and salmon by their mining activities. Many Karuk died of starvation that winter because they had not been able to gather enough provisions.[13]

In December 1854, the *Humboldt Times* reported another attack. This incident, involving a white man and an Indian woman, began a war between the Karuk and the miners. Apparently, a Karuk boy was murdered while protecting his mother from being raped by the white man. The murderer escaped the area, so the Karuk retaliated by killing an ox they believed belonged to the man. Later, after learning that he had sold the ox, the Karuk promised to pay the present owner the price of a steer for it. He refused this, and the miners reacted by attempting to take all the guns from nearby villages. When they met resistance, they attempted to burn the Karuk's houses containing winter provisions.[14]

In early 1855, William M. Young established the Big Bar Rifle Rangers near the mouth of the Trinity River to "protect the citizens of Klamath County" from hostile Indians. On January 5, 1855, Stephan Smith of Big Bend, Oregon, sent a letter to Young, stating that Smith and his men were preparing to attack the Indians there and that they would come down the river to meet Young's Big Bar Rifle Rangers. Their expressed intention was "to exterminate ... the red sons of bitches."[15]

On February 3, 1855, G. A. Flower of Flower's Flat sent a letter to A. M. Rosborough claiming that the Karuk had done harm to the miners and asking the government to supply provisions for a raid. He stated: "We will hunt out the Indians in the vicinity and about the heads of Camp, Rockey, Dillons, and Blue Creeks. ... We will furnish our own arms and clothing all we ask of Government at present is provisions."[16] Military operations that year claimed seventy-five Karuk lives.[17]

A number of Karuk villages were burned in 1856. After countless episodes of violence, such people as Captain Judah and Judge Rosborough were able to help keep law and order in Karuk country. Karuk refugees, finding that their villages had been destroyed, were sometimes given permission to build houses in unoccupied spots near the new white homesteads.

An incredibly cold and harsh winter commenced in 1857, and there were no more incidences of war. In fact, the government passed legislation in which the Indians were to be paid war claims. Representative S. G. Whipple of Klamath County, in southern Oregon, introduced the bill. The amount of $410,000 was paid to the Indians of Siskiyou, Humboldt, and Klamath counties.

Thomas M. Brown became the Klamath County sheriff in 1862, which greatly affected the Karuk since Brown was their good friend. He served as sheriff until 1875.

By 1870, most of the miners had finished reaping the rivers and streams of the Klamath Mountains and hurried on to other regions. A multitude of immigrants followed suit because the once booming economy had slumped. From 1870 through 1890, many miners deserted the Klamath and Salmon rivers, leaving ghost towns and abandoned shacks behind. The Karuk's remote homeland once again became known as "Indian country."

A number of settlers stayed, however, and became merchants, lumbermen, and ranchers. Some of the Anglo men intermarried with the Karuk women and, depending upon the respectability of the family, were accepted into either culture.

In 1887, under the Dawes General Allotment Act, small parcels of land were assigned to the heads of Karuk households and to individual male Indians.[18] Many of the Shasta moved to Happy Camp and Orleans at this time, although a reservation was enacted for them in Scott Valley, east of Karuk country. The Indians felt awkward "owning" land, for they felt the earth was to be used by all, to be taken care of and respected, and not to be owned. As a result of this difference in thinking, many Indians sold their land cheaply, not considering that they owned it in the first place. Later they found themselves homeless. Of forty or more original allotments given to the Karuk along the Klamath River only three are left now.

By the early 1900s, the ancient customs of the Karuk were slowly vanishing. They were becoming acculturated into the mainstream lifestyle. Many ceremonies were no longer performed. Karuk children were forced to attend schools where their cultural customs were suppressed. Some half-breeds, not being accepted into either culture, adopted inferior traits such as abusing alcohol, being greedy, lying, and cheating. The Karuk substituted American material items in place of their own, and sex roles changed as men began to help women make baskets which were sold in stores.

Although the Karuk had few rights, they were expected to obey the white man's laws, such as attending school and learning the ways of "civilized" people. Many Indian children were unable to learn the lore of their parents because of the pressures of living in a new society. The school teachers, usually white and middle class, did not acknowledge the Karuk culture. Besides this, the students were required to wear the formal clothing styles of the Americans, which they considered uncomfortable.

One school teacher, who taught on the Klamath River in the early 1900s, mentioned beautiful gardens made by Karuk families. She claimed that they learned to garden in Federal schools. She also stated that two missionaries came every two weeks to hold a Sunday school at Ka'tim'iin (Somes Bar). These missionaries were sent by the Federal Government to teach religion to a people they considered to be without religion. They then purchased all sorts of Indian handiwork, which they sold as "curios" in eastern cities.[19]

# Endnotes

1. Harry L. Wells, *History of Siskiyou County California*, p. 44.

2. Hazel Davis, "Indian Ned," *Siskiyou Pioneer and Yearbook* (1966), p. 95.

3. Harry L. Wells, *History of Siskiyou County California*, p. 44.

4. Ibid., pp. 55, 59.

5. Ibid., pp. 127-128.

6. Jack Norton, *Genocide in Northwestern California*, p. 38.

7. Ibid., p. 68.

8. Cited in William L. Bright, *Karok* in *Handbook of North American Indians*, R. F. Heizer, ed., vol. 8, p. 189.

9. Edward S. Curtis, *The North American Indian*, vol. 13, p. 58.

10. Cited in Jack Norton, *Genocide in Northwestern California*, p. 6.

11. Ibid., p. 68.

12. A. J. Rosborough, "A. M. Rosborough: Special Indian Agent," *California Historical Society Quarterly*, vol. 26, no. 3, p. 202.

13. Ibid.

14. Jack Norton, *Genocide in Northwestern California*, p. 68.

15. A. J. Rosborough, "A. M. Rosborough: Special Indian Agent," *California Historical Society Quarterly*, vol. 26, no. 3, p. 203.

16. Ibid., p. 204.

17. William L. Bright, *Karok* in *Handbook of North American Indians*, R. F. Heizer, ed., vol. 8, p. 188.

18. Jack Norton, *Genocide in Northwestern California*, p. 113.

19. Eugenia Howells, "Happy Experiences of a Pioneer Teacher in the Wilds of Siskiyou County," *Siskiyou Pioneer and Yearbook* (1971), pp. 28-29.

## Chapter 8

# THE REVIVAL OF A VANISHING CULTURE

In 1848, around 2,700 full-blooded Karuk existed. By 1910, after the disruption caused by the American invaders, only 775 were left.[1] Because they lived in such a remote region, over a quarter of the Karuk survived the American invasion. The Shasta, who bordered the Karuk to the east, were decimated to such an extent that only one out of twenty members remained in 1910. Other tribes perished completely.

By 1948, scarcely two dozen elderly full-blooded Karuk who followed the ancient ways remained.[2] There were some of mixed blood, however, who had learned the Karuk traditions. One woman, whose father was a stagecoach driver (an Irishman) and whose mother was a full-blooded Karuk, stated that when she was a young girl in Orleans, the white people never came around her. Although she knew English, there was no reason to speak it until she was twenty. At this time, in the early 1930s, she entered the "white man's world" as a lumberman's wife.

Today, the Karuk live not only in the Klamath Mountains but also in Scott Valley, in the Shasta Valley, on the coast in Humboldt and Trinity counties, and in other areas of California and Oregon. Some reside in other parts of the United States and overseas. Most Karuk have moved due to their acculturation by such American institutions as school and government, and because there is little means of economic advancement along the Klamath River.

All Native Americans in the United States were declared citizens and given the right to vote in 1924.[3] In 1929, Charles J. Rhoads and Henry Scattergood were appointed to head the Office of Indian Affairs. These two men laid the groundwork for the Indian Reorganization Act enacted in 1934 by the Roosevelt Administration.[4]

This act gave Native Americans many legal rights. From this time on, the natural resources of tribal lands were to be conserved and protected. Native Americans could now defend their civil and property rights in court, advanced schooling was made more attainable to those desiring it, and job priority was given to Indians within the agencies that served them. The government also set up a fund from which incorporated tribes could borrow for individual or community purposes.

In 1951, the Wozencraft Treaty was passed by the United States government. This agreement promised to pay a compensation to all Native Americans and their descendants who resided in the state of California on July 1, 1852. A census was then authorized to determine eligibility.[5]

This government compensation has aided the Karuk to revive some of their customs. Ceremonies were held at Inaam in the 1950s and at Ka'tim'iin in 1970, but they were shortened because the medicine men had no time to practice the full ritual exercises and lacked complete knowledge of the ceremonial features. Some of the Karuk refused to participate because the ceremonies lacked tradition and were funded in part with government aid.[6]

Today, the Karuk hold all of their ancient ceremonies with expenses met by donations from their own pockets. But many of their valuable treasures and ornaments are no longer available. They are locked up in museums and in individual collections, and the Karuk have no access to them. Many of the ceremonial sites have been destroyed by construction, forestry, and agricultural projects. Forestry workers, highway crews, and tourists continue to violate them.[7]

*Photo 23. Group attending the marking of the Karuk ceremonial site at Clear Creek. Left to right: Francis Davis (medicine man), Wes Hamilton, Shirley White, Vera Arwood, Mrs. Francis Davis, and Daisy Jacobs.*

## The Karuk Tribe of California[8]

The Karuk lifestyle has changed drastically since the 1850s—from a Stone Age culture to a modern industrial one. While losing much of their traditional identity, the Karuk have accepted, on the other hand, the use of household appliances, cars, supermarkets, and other aspects of modern California living.

Generations of Native Americans, suppressed by society, have been discouraged from using their native language and held back from following their ancestral lifestyles. However, since the civil rights movement of the 1960s, the constitutional rights and privileges of Native Americans and other minorities have been extended and protected.

To preserve traditional knowledge among the Upriver People, the Karuk Tribe of California was incorporated in 1965, funded by benefits from the Economic Development Act. Any person one-eighth Karuk or more may join. This organization assists many Karuk spiritually, educationally, and financially.

During the organization's early days, a number of feuds occurred among its officiating members. The location of meetings and responsibilities of the board members were heatedly discussed. However, in 1979 the disagreement came to an end when the Tribe approved the formation of a governing body and began to vote candidates into office.

This governing body consisted of two elected councils—the Orleans District Council and the Happy Camp District Council. Each group met once a month on a different Wednesday. In 1985, the two councils were merged into one, and it became known as the Karuk Tribal Council. Any member of the Karuk community is welcome to attend its meetings. Among other services, the Council distributes a newsletter to inform readers about tribal politics, employment opportunities, training and health care programs, and local news.

An important responsibility of the organization is to support civil rights legislation that protects the expressions of Indian traditions and lifestyles. People with technical skills, college educations, and knowledge gained from their elders now manage tribal programs and fight legal battles. Under this leadership, two court cases, one concerning fishing rights on the Klamath River and the other over the protection of sacred lands, have been fought during the last decade.

## Fishing Rights

An ever present problem among the Karuk is the right to fish on the Klamath River. The Federal Government banned traditional gill netting in 1979 because the Indians sold fish commercially—often for a living—causing a severe decline in the river's salmon and steelhead population. This was destructive to the ecological balance of the Klamath and Salmon rivers.

*Photo 24. Madeline Davis with samples of her basketry caps.*

After numerous court cases on the issue, a decision was reached that established a new conservation program in which millions of fish were bred in small pond sites and released into the Klamath River. Funding for this program came from the Department of Fish and Game, the Bureau of Indian Affairs, and the Northern California Development Program.

The final verdict of the case came in 1985. The Karuk can now dip net at Ishi Pishi Falls and those with valid permits can gill net and hunt for ceremonial purposes from Ishi Pishi Falls to the mouth of the Klamath River. According to a representative of the Karuk tribe, however, obtaining valid permits remains a problem because the government has not issued any since the verdict was reached.

## Saving Sacred Country

Another legal battle pursued in the 1980s was with the United States Forest Service, who wanted to both log and build a road through 26,000 acres of sacred high country surrounding Chimney Rock in northwestern California. Located in the Six Rivers National Forest, this land includes the watersheds of Blue Creek and Eightmile Creek, which flow into the Klamath River. For generations the Karuk, the Tolowa, and the Yurok Indians have journeyed to this alpine wilderness for ceremonial purposes.

At first the courts decided in favor of the Karuk and other northwestern California tribes. Based on the First Amendment's protection of religious expression, it was decided that the construction of the road and the subsequent logging would destroy the privacy and silence of the sacred wilderness and interfere with religious rituals and ceremonies. After a long battle, the case was finally brought before the Supreme Court of the United States, where it was revoked in 1988. This was a setback to the protection of Native American religious rights.

## The Romantic Movement

Before the civil rights movement began, the Karuk could not have attempted to win such cases in court, much less have the legal access to fight for their rights. They were often shunned and thought of as inferior because they dressed and acted in a particular manner. Consequently, many Karuk began to dress and act like the mainstream culture, forgetting their ancestor's precious ways.

Fortunately, there were some who did not let their native culture vanish. These individuals often had to live double lives, following traditional practices at home but outwardly blending in with the rest of society. Today, these traditionalists are respected as tribal "elders."

A few Karuk elders have been honored and commended for their knowledge and the hard work they have put forth to revive their culture. Shan Davis, medicine man and honorary language teacher, not only worked day and night to create a language manual, he also revived many ancient ceremonies. Madeline Davis, an expert basketweaver, has taught traditional weaving techniques as well as other secrets of her culture. Her daughter, Priscilla Ainsworth, language teacher and social worker, is following in her mother's footsteps. Julian Lang has visited different institutions throughout northern California, lecturing and presenting slide shows on the Karuk way of life.

Members of the Karuk Tribal Council have joined with these elders to institute projects related to the Karuk culture. Courses such as the Karuk language, basketry, and bread-making are being taught at schools in northwestern California. The Karuk-Beartooth Wilderness School is now offered seasonally in the Klamath Mountains as part of the renewal movement. Children, youth, and adults camp out in the forest, living together in tepees for ten days. Guides use their skills and knowledge to help their students look for basketry materials, gather acorns, and do other traditional chores and games. Skills learned include fire-making using a traditional bow drill, identification and preparation of edible and medicinal plants, shelter construction, and primitive craftswork.

With the support of the Council and the knowledge and skills of the elders, many youth are becoming more interested in their native culture. Although new practices have been introduced, such as bread-making and camping in tepees, most things sponsored by the Council are authentic. If more people participate in these programs, they will help to preserve an important part of American aboriginal culture, for the United States is first and foremost North American Indian country. If Native Americans lose their traditions, America will lose an important part of its identity.

Being relatives, the Karuk have always stayed together wherever they go. At playing baseball, participating in and attending community events, or enjoying American holidays with more buoyancy than Anglos themselves, they are a

*Photo 25. Sara Nesbitt in traditional dress, holding an Indian plate. Also shown are storage baskets and a basketry cap.*

family. But, at these games and events, at dances and at fairs, some of the Upriver People drink excessively and end up getting arrested. Alcohol and drug abuse is a problem that continues to harm the well-being of the Karuk community.

The Karuk community has a tremendous support system that can bring friendship and positive feelings to all who participate in it. Traditional ceremonies, hand games, stick games, and card games, not to mention Bingo, as well as potlucks and other gatherings, are held in which the Karuk people from all walks of life come together, have a good time, and watch or participate in the day's events. Fundraising events for these and other festivities are held throughout the year.

The Karuk Tribe of California also aids people in need financially. When one family lost most of their possessions in a house fire, the Tribe not only gave them money, but food and other necessities as well. They have built houses for poor families; provided health services to families with chil-

*Photo 26. Glen Davis and Benji Camarena preparing for the White Deerskin Ceremony, holding large flint. Ka'tim'iin September 1989.*

dren, the sick, and the elderly; and helped many Karuk youths and adults acquire jobs. The Karuk Tribal Council community center, located in Happy Camp, posts job opportunities available in the Klamath River area throughout the year.

The Karuk Tribe of California is doing all it can to revive the ancient culture. They have managed to preserve many important Karuk customs and practices. It is my hope that it will continue to play a large part in preserving Karuk identity in the future.

## Endnotes

1. William L. Bright, *Karok* in *Handbook of North American Indians*, R. F. Heizer, ed., p. 189.

2. Ibid.

3. Raphael, *The Indian Today: The Book of American Indians*, p. 143.

4. Ibid.

5. Ibid.

6. Gary B. Palmer, *Karok World Renewal and Village Sites*, p. 16.

7. Ibid.

8. Information based upon interviews with the Karuk Tribal Council, papers, and tribal newsletters.

# Appendix

# SOME KARUK MYTHS

## How Pain Came into the World[1]

Pee-naaf-fich [Pihnêefich], the Coyote, heard of a country where no one lived except bad people who loved to hurt folks. So he said to the Eagle, "Let us go and kill all the bad people in this distant valley we hear about."

So he and the Eagle started out. They traveled and traveled till they came to a valley thick with houses and full of people. It was nighttime when they got there.

They went into a house, and there were many  people sitting about. They talked in a friendly way to the Coyote and Eagle, and invited them to sleep. But they knew better than to go to sleep in such a place.

So the Coyote said: "We don't feel sleepy. We feel so good we would like to make a big dance. Let us go outside and build a big fire and dance."

Now it is a great thing to watch at a dance, and so while the visitors made a big fire and painted for the dance, all the people of the place began to gather together to watch. They sent word everywhere, and by the time the fun began all the houses were empty all over the valley, and the people were hurrying to where the flames were shooting up in the midst of the village.

First the Coyote began to dance. Then the Eagle began to dance. The Coyote leaped and the Eagle flew; and both sang and danced, and sang and danced. It was hard to tell which danced the higher. It grew late in the night, and they kept on singing and dancing, and singing and dancing, and all the people sat still and watched. No one had ever looked on at a dance half so fine.

After a while it grew cloudy up in the sky. Towards midnight snow began to fall. All the people just watched and watched.

It snowed and snowed, and snowed—dark snow, thick in the air. The Eagle and the Coyote danced higher still. All the people watched.

Soon the snow was up to the people's knees. Then it was up to their hips. No one could quit watching the dance. Then towards morning a big frost came.

The Eagle and Coyote just danced, and danced, and danced. The frost grew so thick it was like a crust of ice. When it was morning, and light enough to see, the two dancers saw they could stop and rest. They rested beside the burnt-out fire. And all around them the people clustered, watching and watching. They sat straight and never lifted an arm, even when the dance was finished. They were all wide-eyed and staring, and no company ever sat so still. They were corpses, frozen in the snow.

The Coyote and the Eagle went around among them, laughing and tapping each one on the head, to see if there was one alive. Then they danced a little more for joy, for they thought that in a single night the whole tribe of wicked people was killed off.

But there was one that they didn't know about, who had crawled off to a house when he first began to freeze. The Eagle and Coyote left the valley without finding him, and boasted to all they met about what they had done. And this one man who was left recovered, and has ever since been working out vengeance for his people. He is Pain, and he never visits you but you suffer. Sometimes he kills, but usually he prefers to take his pleasure out of people first, so that really it seems as if it would have been better had the Coyote and the Eagle left the wicked people undisturbed. For those were the days before the change in the world, when no man felt any torment, and a man could even be killed and not suffer.

# Bluejay Medicine Man[2]

Ukniii ... Chipmunk was sick all the time. So they went to fetch Bluejay. They always paid him with chestnuts. So he was treating him. Then he said, "I cannot cure him! I can't do any more for him!" Then he said, "Go and fetch Hummingbird!" Then Bluejay and Hummingbird were treating him together. He got well, and they said, "We treated him quite hard." Now he was up and around, he was getting well nicely. Then he got sick again. So they said, "You had better go and fetch Bluejay again." Again he treated him. They paid him with chestnuts, a panful of chestnuts. So he treated him. Then he said, "I cannot do any more for him, you better fetch someone else!" They said, "You had better call Hummingbird again!" Then they fetched him. He came. He treated him. Then Bluejay sat down. Now that fellow Hummingbird was dancing the medicine dance, but Bluejay was still sitting there. Then Hummingbird sang, "Some time ago it was done by trickery," as he was dancing. Then he said, "My mouth is small!" Then Bluejay said, "Indeed! Maybe he will say something!" Then Hummingbird said, "Bluejay does not know his medicine!" Then he said, "katch-katch-katch-katch," and up through the smokehole he flew out of the house. That one kept on poisoning Chipmunk, because he liked chestnut mush. Therefore he poisoned Chipmunk. He was paid much chestnut mush for treating him. Therefore he poisoned him. That is all.

# How Salmon Was Given to Mankind[2]

(Humanity has not yet arrived upon the scene of this world. There are people living about, but they are half-men and half-gods, the precursors of mankind, still animals. It is also to be born in mind that "salmon", their chief food, is equivalent to our "bread.")

At Amweykyara ("salmon-fishing-place") there lived two girls.

These girls always had plenty of salmon to eat. People were always visiting them. "Where do you get your fish?"

They would have liked to know, but they never could find out. The girls gave their visitors salmon, and the guests relished it.

Meanwhile, at Katimin (the center of the Karuk world) there lived a spirit-man. He thought, "I think I had better go there and find out where they get their salmon...I am sure I'll find out!" So he started. He slung his quiver on his back. He arrived at Utiha-pishahnaamitch ("Where-they-wash-flint"). There he got some alder-bark. He chipped it off (the inner bark, when exposed to the air, looks red or salmon colour), he fixed the pieces nicely and put them in his quiver. Then he started down the river.

He got to Tahye'maka. That's where the two girls had their house. They called out to him, "Come in!" and when he got in he looked, and lo and behold! all around there were slabs of salmon hanging.

Well, and finally they cooked some salmon, and then they ate.

Then the one who had come he reached into his quiver, and he said, "I also will eat my lunch!" and as they were looking at him he took out his salmon and ate it.

They looked at each other, the two sisters. They were wondering where he got it. When he got through eating, he went and sat down outside. The girls started to talk, "Where do you suppose he gets this salmon? Oh! and we thought that no one would ever find out!"

Then he decided that he was going to stop there that night. So they said to him, "All right, you can sleep over there in the sweathouse (the man's club)." But he said, "No indeed! I'll sleep right here!" So they said, "All right!", and they went and brought in lots of wood for the fire. Then they all went to bed. He who had come, he slept on one side of the fire.

After a while one of the girls said, "I do think he is asleep for good!" They had built a roaring fire and he never moved. Then one of them got up. She removed a plank from the wall, she picked up a pole and she poked around for a while. She poked around and the water made a splashing noise. It was the salmon. Then they said, "It's enough with two!" Then they went out. They went down to Situmuknaamitch ("mice-pond"), and there they took two salmon out of the water.

But he who was lying inside, the moment they went out he jumped up. He picked up the pole. He poked around. He poked and poked. The salmon were overflowing. They flowed over. They ran out upstream to Havisharasuf Creek. From there they escaped into the Klamath River.

And the girls they were wondering, "What's the matter? The water is making so much noise!" They came back and went in, and lo and behold! he who had come he was already gone. And when they looked into their fishing-place it was empty as well. Then they thought, "How mean of him to have spoiled it thus for us! And we who thought that no one would ever find out where we got the salmon. Well, then, we had better metamorphose ourselves."

And then they decided, "When humanity arrives, let them feed on the salmon that are now swarming in the Klamath River."

Then they picked up their large storing-baskets and they went across the river. They climbed up onto a long ridge, and they travelled along the ridge, down stream and at last they stopped.

From downhill they could hear the confused noise of humanity who had come to live. Then they covered themselves with their huge baskets, and they cried, "Right here we are going to metamorphose ourselves. That man, he is already back at Katimin, he who spoiled it for us."

He had spoilt it for them because he was thinking, "Salmon I want for myself in my own Falls" (at Katimin, the center of the world).

And to this day you can see the two white rocks standing right there where they metamorphosed themselves, the girls.

That's all.

## Endnotes

1.  From M. B. Denny, "Orleans Indian Legends," *Out West*, vol. 25, no. 1 (July 1906).

2.  Translated by J. de Angulo and L. S. Freeman in "Karok Texts," *International Journal of American Linguistics*, vol. 6, nos. 3-4 (1931).

# BIBLIOGRAPHY

Arnold, Mary E. and Mabel Reed. *In the Land of the Grass-hopper Song.* Lincoln: University of Nebraska Press, 1980.

Balfrey, Stanley J. *History of the Schools of Siskiyou County.* Siskiyou County Board of Education, n.d.

Bright, William L. "Some Place Names on the Klamath River." *Western Folklore,* vol. 11, no. 2 (1952):121-122.

_____. *The Karok Language.* University of California Publications in Linguistics, vol. 13. Berkeley: University of California Press, 1957.

_____. "Karok Names." *Names,* vol. 8, no. 3 (1958):172-179.

Chartkoff, Joseph L. and Kerry K. Chartkoff. "Late Period Settlement of the Middle Klamath River of Northwest California." *American Antiquity,* vol. 40, no. 2 (1975):172-179.

_____. *The Archaeology of California.* Stanford: Stanford University Press, 1984.

Cook, Sherburne F. *The Conflict Between the California Indian and White Civilization.* Berkeley: University of California Press, 1976.

_____. *The Aboriginal Population of the North Coast of California.* University of California Anthropological Records, vol. 16, no. 3. Berkeley: University of California Press, 1956.

Curtis, Edward S. *The North American Indian,* vol. 13. Cambridge: The University Press, 1924.

Davis, James T. *Trade Routes and Economic Exchange Among the Indians of California.* Reports of the University of California Archaeological Survey, no. 54. Berkeley: University of California Press, 1961.

De Angulo, J. and L. S. Freeland. "Karok Texts." *International Journal of American Linguistics,* vol. 6, nos. 3-4 (1931):194-226.

Denny, M. B. "Orleans Indian Legends." *Out West,* vol. 25, no. 1 (1906-07).

Driver, Harold E. *Culture Element Distributions: Northwest California.* University of California Anthropological Records, vol. 1, no. 6. Berkeley: University of California Press, 1939.

Drucker, Philip. *A Karok World-Renewal Ceremony at Panaminik.* University of California Publications in American Archaeology and Ethnology, vol. 35, no. 3. Berkeley: University of California Press, 1943.

Eargle Jr., Dolan H. *The Earth is Our Mother: A Guide to the Indians of California, Their Locales and Historic Sites.* San Francisco: Tree Company Press, 1986.

Gifford, Edward W. *Karok Field Notes,* Part 1. (Ethnological Document no. 174 in Department and Museum of Anthropology, University of California; ms. in University Archives, Bancroft Library, Berkeley) 1939.

_____. *Karok Field Notes,* Part 2. (Ethnological Document no. 179 in Department and Museum of Anthropology, University of California; ms. in University Archives, Bancroft Library, Berkeley) 1940.

Gould, Richard A. *Archaeology of the Point Saint George Site and Tolowa Prehistory.* University of California Publications in Anthropology, vol. 4. Berkeley: University of California Press, 1966.

_____. *A Radiocarbon Date from Point St. George Site, Northwestern California.* Contributions of the University of California Archaeological Research Facility, vol. 14. Berkeley: University of California Press, 1972.

Harrington, John P. "Karuk Texts." *International Journal of American Linguistics*, vol. 6, no. 2 (1931):121-161.

_____. *Tobacco Among the Karuk Indians of California.* Bureau of American Ethnology, Bulletin 94. Washington: Smithsonian Institution, 1932.

Harrington, M. R. *An Ancient Site at Borax Lake, California.* Southern Museum Papers, no. 16. Los Angeles: 1948.

Hart, John. *Hiking the Bigfoot Country: Exploring the Wildlands of Northern California and Southern Oregon.* San Francisco: Sierra Club, 1975.

Hawkins, S. and D. Bleything. *Getting Off on Ninety-Six and Other Less Traveled Roads.* Beaverton, Oregon: The Touchstone Press, 1975.

Heizer, R. F. *A Bibliography of Ancient Man in California.* University of California Archaeological Survey Reports, no. 2. Berkeley: University of California Press, 1948.

_____. "The California Indians: Archaeology, Varieties of Culture, Arts of Life." *California Historical Society Quarterly*, vol. 41, no. 1 (1962):1-28.

_____, editor. *George Gibb's Journal of Redick McKee's Expedition through Northwestern California in 1851.* Archaeological Research Facility. Berkeley: University of California Press, 1972.

_____, editor. *Handbook of North American Indians*, vol. 8. Washington: Smithsonian Institution, 1978.

_____, editor. *They Were Only Diggers: A Collection of Articles from California Newspapers, 1851 - 1866, on Indian and White Relations.* Ramona, California: Ballena Press, 1974.

_____ and A. B. Elsasser. *The Natural World of the California Indians.* Berkeley: University of California Press, 1980.

_____ and M. A. Whipple, editors. *The California Indians: A Source Book,* 2nd ed. Berkeley: University of California Press, 1971.

Hodge, F. W., editor. *Handbook of American Indians North of Mexico,* vol. 1. Bureau of American Ethnology, Bulletin 30. Washington: Smithsonian Institution, 1912.

Jones, J. Roy. *Saddle Bags in Siskiyou.* Yreka, California: News-Journal Print Shop, 1953.

Karuk Tribal Council, Happy Camp, California 96039.

Kelly, Isabel T. *The Carver's Art of the Indians of Northwestern California.* University of California Publications in American Archaeology and Ethnology, vol. 24, no. 7. Berkeley: University of California Press, 1930.

Kroeber, A. L. "A Ghost Dance in California." *Journal of American Folklore,* vol. 17, no. 64 (1904):32-35.

_____. "A Karok Orpheus Myth." *Journal of American Folklore,* vol. 59, no. 231 (1945):13-19.

_____. *Basket Designs of the Indians of Northwestern California.* University of California Publications in American Archaeology and Ethnology, vol. 2, no. 4. Berkeley: The University Press, 1905.

_____. *California Culture Provinces.* University of California Publications in American Archaeology and Ethnology, vol. 17, no. 2. Berkeley: University of California Press, 1920.

_____. *Handbook of the Indians of California.* Bureau of American Ethnology, Bulletin 78. Washington: Smithsonian Institution, 1925.

_____. *Karok Towns.* University of California Publications in American Archaeology and Ethnology, vol. 35, no. 4. Berkeley: University of California Press, 1936.

_____. *Types of Indian Culture in California.* University of California Publications in American Archaeology and Ethnology, vol. 2, no. 3. Berkeley: The University Press, 1905.

_____ and Edward W. Gifford. *Karok Myths.* Berkeley: University of California Press, 1980.

_____ and Edward W. Gifford. *World Renewal: A Cult System of Native Northwest California.* University of California Anthropological Records, vol. 13, no. 1. Berkeley: University of California Press, 1949.

_____ and S. A. Barrett. *Fishing Among the Indians of Northwestern California.* University of California Anthropological Records, vol. 21, nos. 1-2. Berkeley: University of California Press, 1962.

Kroeber, Theodora and R. F. Heizer. *Almost Ancestors: The First Californians.* San Francisco: Sierra Club, 1968.

Lantis, David W., Rodney Steiner, and Arthur E. Karinen. *California: Land of Contrast.* Dubuque, Iowa: Kendall/Hunt Publishing Company, 1977.

Leonardy, F. *The Archaeology of a Late Prehistoric Village in Northwestern California.* University of Oregon Museum of Natural History, Bulletin 4. Eugene: University of Oregon, 1967.

Meighan, C. W. and C. V. Haynes. "The Borax Lake Site Revisited." *Science,* vol. 167, no. 3922 (1970):1213-1221.

Merriam, C. Hart. *Ethnographic Notes on California Indian Tribes, II. Ethnological Notes on Northern and Southern California Indian Tribes,* comp. and ed. R. F. Heizer. Reports of the University of California

Archaeological Survey, no. 68. Berkeley: University of California Archaeological Research Facility, 1967.

_____. "The Indian Population of California." *American Anthropology*, vol. 7, no. 4 (1905):594-606.

Moratto, Michael J. *California Archaeology.* Orlando: Academic Press, 1984.

Norton, Jack. *Genocide in Northwestern California.* San Francisco: The Indian Historian Press, 1979.

Oakeshott, Gordon B. *California's Changing Landscapes: A Guide to the Geology of the State.* San Francisco: McGraw-Hill Book Company, 1971.

O'Neale, Lila M. *Yurok-Karok Basket Weavers.* University of California Publications in American Archaeology and Ethnology, vol. 32, no. 1. Berkeley: University of California Press, 1932.

Palmer, Gary B. *Karok World Renewal and Village Sites: A Cultural and Historical District.* (Unpublished manuscript in California State University, Chico, Northeastern California collection) 1980.

Powers, Stephen. *Tribes of California.* Berkeley: University of California Press, 1976. (Reprint of 1877 edition.)

Raphael. *The Indian Today: The Book of American Indians.* A Fawcett Book, no. 191. 1953.

Rosborough, Alex J. "A. M. Rosborough: Special Indian Agent." *California Historical Society Quarterly*, vol. 26, no. 3 (1947):201-207.

Sample, L. L. *Trade and Trails in Aboriginal California.* University of California Archaeological Survey Reports, no. 8. Berkeley: University of California Press, 1950.

Schenck, Sara M. and Edward W. Gifford. *Karok Ethnobotany.* University of California Anthropological Records, vol. 13, no. 6. Berkeley: University of California Press, 1952.

*Siskiyou Pioneer and Yearbook,* vol. 3, no. 9. Yreka, California: Siskiyou County Historical Society, 1966.

*Siskiyou Pioneer and Yearbook,* vol. 4, no. 4. Yreka, California: Siskiyou County Historical Society, 1971.

Wallace, David R. *The Klamath Knot: Explorations of Myth and Evolution.* San Francisco: Sierra Club, 1983.

Wells, Harry L. *History of Siskiyou County, California.* Oakland, California: D. J. Stewart and Company, 1881.